GRACE WALK
DEVOTIONAL

Steve McVey

HARVEST HOUSE PUBLISHERS
EUGENE, OREGON

Unless otherwise indicated, all Scripture quotations are from the New American Standard Bible®, ©
1960, 1962, 1963, 1968, 1971, 1972, 1973, 1975, 1977, 1995 by The Lockman Foundation. Used by permission. (www.Lockman.org)

Verses marked NLT are taken from first edition of the *Holy Bible,* New Living Translation, copyright ©
1996. Used by permission of Tyndale House Publishers, Inc., Wheaton, IL 60189 USA. All rights reserved.

Verses marked NIV are taken from The Holy Bible, New International Version® NIV®. Copyright © 1973,
1978, 1984, 2011 by Biblica, Inc.™ Used by permission. All rights reserved worldwide.

Verses marked KJV are taken from the King James Version of the Bible.

Verses marked MSG are taken from The Message. Copyright © by Eugene H. Peterson 1993, 1994, 1995,
1996, 2000, 2001, 2002. Used by permission of NavPress Publishing Group.

Verses marked GNT are taken from the Good News Translation – Second Edition © 1992 by American
Bible Society. Used by permission.

Verses marked ESV are from The ESV® Bible (The Holy Bible, English Standard Version), copyright ©
2001 by Crossway Bibles, a publishing ministry of Good News Publishers. Used by permission. All rights
reserved.

Verses marked NLT 2004 are taken from second edition of the *Holy Bible,* New Living Translation, copyright © 1996, 2004. Used by permission of Tyndale House Publishers, Inc., Wheaton, IL 60189 USA.
All rights reserved.

Emphasis (italics) in Scripture quotations has been added by the author.

Cover by Left Coast Design, Portland, Oregon

Cover photo © Len Green / Shutterstock

THE GRACE WALK DEVOTIONAL
Copyright © 2013 by Steve McVey
Published by Harvest House Publishers
Eugene, Oregon 97402
www.harvesthousepublishers.com

Library of Congress Cataloging-in-Publication Data
    McVey, Steve, 1954-
    The grace walk devotional / Steve McVey.
        p. cm.
    ISBN 978-0-7369-5345-0 (pbk.)
    ISBN 978-0-7369-5346-7 (eBook)
    1. Christian life—Meditations. I. Title.
    BV4501.3.M395 2013
    242—dc23
                                                                        2012026066

Printed in the United States of America
            12 13 14 15 16 17 18 19 20 / LB-NI / 10 9 8 7 6 5 4 3 2 1

Contents

The Way of Grace 5

1. A Biblical Case for Optimism 9
2. Having Eyes to See 13
3. A Busy Mind 17
4. A Job Well Done 21
5. Letting Go 25
6. Childlike Faith 29
7. Christ, Our Anchor 33
8. Cling to Jesus 35
9. Dead Pods and New Life 37
10. Don't Touch the Cactus 41
11. A Friendly Universe 45
12. Looking for a Revival 49
13. Watering Down the Gospel 53
14. Does Grace Encourage Sin? 57
15. Looking in the Wrong Places 61
16. Making Promises to God 65
17. Distorted Motivation 69
18. Making a Difference Behind the Scenes 73
19. Abandoning the Religious Rat Race 77
20. Absurd Forgiveness 81
21. Golf and Grace 83
22. Shame—A Silly Game 87
23. Trusting Our Hearts 91
24. Love Changes Everything 95
25. We're Not in Kansas Anymore 99
26. Making Music Together 103
27. Canned Foods and Closed Hearts 107

28. Your Father Will Care for You 111
29. Faith and Candy Bars 115
30. Compassionate Gentleness 119
31. Dead Things 123
32. Dealing with Our Fears 127
33. Dealing with Sins in Our Lives 131
34. Disguising Doubts as Belief 135
35. True Value 139
36. Don't Give Up! 143
37. Eyes That See 147
38. The Offense of Grace 149
39. Forgiving Ourselves 153
40. Getting Along with Other People 157
41. Sometimes God Works in
    Not-So-Mysterious Ways 161
42. Who Is Qualified? 165
43. Hearing God's Voice 169
44. Holy Hugs 173
45. Hurricanes and Jugglers 177
46. Living in Freedom 181
47. Rest Awhile 185
48. Holy Work 189
49. Accepting Divine Forgiveness 193
50. Surviving the Storms 195
51. Let's Dance 199
52. Dare to Live Your Dream 203
53. Making Our Days Count 207
54. Norman Rockwell Expectations
    in a Homer Simpson World 211
55. The Truth Sets You Free 213
56. Wounded Soldiers 217
57. Monkey Gods 221
58. The Danger of Drifting 225
59. A Subtle Form of Idolatry 229
60. The Value of Laughter 233

The Way of Grace

An everyday lifestyle that is consistent with our faith isn't something that naturally fits contemporary culture. In a pluralistic society like ours, where many people are developing an increasing distaste for anything that even hints at religion, how is a believer to live so the people in our sphere of influence are impacted by divine love…and aren't turned off by what they perceive as nothing more than another religious person's perspective?

The answer is grace. Walking in grace is very different from living religiously. When we attempt to live a religious lifestyle we focus on doing the right things so we can please God. We focus on how we are acting in our everyday circumstances. Plain and simple, religion focuses on behavior.

The way of grace is very different. It's not that our actions don't matter when we walk in grace. They do—but the difference is that the grace walk isn't centered on doing the right things. Instead, it finds its motivation in the love we have for our God and for the people around us. Instead of revolving around a religious performance, the grace walk is about personal relationships—our relationship to God and to others.

Jesus once talked about how we are to be the salt of the earth. A life lived in grace causes those we meet to become thirsty for the Water of Life, Christ Himself. The amazing thing about the grace walk is that, when we understand what it means, we discover that it is an effortless lifestyle. We stop struggling to do the right things so we can make our spiritual mark on the world. We simply relax, be our authentic selves, and allow the love of God to flow through us in a natural and unforced way. As we do that, people are attracted to the One they see in us.

Perhaps one of the greatest benefits of the grace walk is that we stop living with the constant self-introspection that is created when our lifestyle is motivated by religious duty instead of love. Most people know that heavy, internal sense that they haven't done enough to please God. Religious introspection is characterized by a constant awareness of where we think we have failed. Grace takes that away by causing us to realize that God doesn't set some standard we're expected to meet. He simply wants us to relax and let Him be who He is in and through us.

Jesus calls us to a lifestyle of calm confidence in Him, not one of frantic fear that we need to do more so that we can be more. He described the grace walk in Matthew 11:28-30. Here's how *The Message* paraphrases it:

> Are you tired? Worn out? Burned out on religion? Come to me. Get away with me and you'll recover your life. I'll show you how to take a real rest. Walk with me and work with me—watch how I do it. Learn the unforced rhythms of grace. I won't lay anything heavy or ill-fitting on you. Keep company with me and you'll learn to live freely and lightly.

Jesus' words perfectly describe the grace walk. *The Grace Walk Devotional* was written to help you experience what it means to live the lifestyle He described. If you've tried to live in a way that honors God only to consistently be more aware of your shortcomings than your progress, this book is going to help you.

If your spiritual life seems to have been driven by self-discipline and determination to do the right thing, you're going to love it when you discover what it means to live in a way that honors Him simply by being yourself. Your Father created you and lives in you. As your mind is renewed through these devotional thoughts, you will learn how the unforced rhythms of grace produce an internal rest while at the same time making an external impact on people to a degree you haven't known until now.

The Grace Walk Devotional is intended to encourage you by showing you how to live the life you were created to enjoy without a struggle. You'll gain the most benefit if you read one chapter each day. Read each chapter prayerfully. Then, as you go through your day, ask the Holy Spirit to work into your life what you've understood as you read the devotion. Watch the way He puts into practice the things He is teaching you through this book. The best part is that it will happen naturally, without a struggle on your part.

The grace walk is the life your Father intends for you to know. Go forward through the chapters of this book with anticipation. You will encounter the One who loves you more than any other as you read these chapters. Then, having encountered Him, you will experience His divine love flowing through you and affecting everybody around you.

1

A Biblical Case for Optimism

The path of the righteous is like the light of dawn,
That shines brighter and brighter until the full day.

—Proverbs 4:18

What do you see when you look down the road of life? The foundation for optimism is Jesus Christ. Faith in Him is the conduit through which He is able to pour out into your life all the good He has planned for you to be, to have, and to do. It all boils down to one simple question: Do you believe that God wants you to experience and enjoy His blessings? Jesus once said, "It shall be done to you according to your faith" (Matthew 9:29). It is important for you to believe in God's goodness and know that you are a recipient of that goodness.

As you look down the path that lies ahead for you, do you anticipate good things from God? Do you expect things to become better or worse? Make no mistake about it—what we believe about God's working in our lives in this area has an inestimable effect on how we move forward and what we will experience and enjoy in the coming days.

Israel wandered in the wilderness for 40 years, although the journey from Egypt to Canaan should have taken only 11 days. Why did it take them so long to enter into the Promised Land? The Bible says, "They were not able to enter because of unbelief" (Hebrews 3:19). With paradise only 11 days away, they lived in self-imposed misery for 40 years, all because they refused to believe God.

How long have you wandered in circles? Maybe, like Israel, you've been in the wilderness for many years. God says through Isaiah that it's time for you to accept and appropriate *good* news. Get ready because good news has arrived. Your Father is bringing you out of the wilderness.

What do you see when you look down the path that lies ahead? Will you believe what God says about it? He says, "The path of the righteous is like the light of dawn, that shines brighter and brighter until the full day." The good news is that you *are* righteous! Jesus Christ has made you righteous.

Romans 5:17 tells us, "If by the transgression of the one, death reigned through the one, much more those who receive the abundance of grace and of the gift of righteousness will reign in life through the One, Jesus Christ." Righteousness is not something earned by good behavior. The Bible calls it "the gift of righteousness" in this verse. The verse assures you that if you will receive this reality you will *reign* in life! Does that sound like a biblical reason for optimism?

Second Corinthians 5:21 says, "He made Him who knew no sin to be sin on our behalf, so that we might become the righteousness of God in Him." Jesus took your sin upon Himself so that you can now enjoy His righteousness as your own. The fact that you are righteous gives you reason to know that your path is like the dawn that will only become brighter and brighter!

Jesus Christ in you is the gateway to an eternally bright future. There is no reason to be anything but positive! Consider what the Bible says: "Be strong and take courage, all you who put your hope in the LORD! …The LORD delights in those…who put their hope in His unfailing love…Surely you have a future ahead of you; your hope will not be disappointed…'I know the plans that I have for you,' saith the LORD, 'they are plans for good and not disaster, to give you a future and a hope'…There is hope for your future."*

Will you believe what Scripture says and trust the indwelling Christ to bring it to pass in your circumstances? You have the enabling grace of Jesus Christ within you to live a supernatural life. Will you accept and appropriate the good news? Will you lay hold of the hope of fulfilling the God-given dreams of your heart?

---

* Respectively: Psalm 31:24 NLT; Psalm 147:11 NIV; Proverbs 23:18 NLT; Jeremiah 29:11 KJV; Jeremiah 31:17.

The apostle Paul did. He wrote triumphantly, "Now glory be to God! By His mighty power at work within us, He is able to accomplish infinitely more than we would ever dare to ask or hope!" (Ephesians 3:20 NLT).

Regardless of how your circumstances may look right now, don't give up on God! You will certainly experience some trying days, but He is with you in them. So don't lose hope. Look ahead with a hope energized by grace. "Without wavering, let us hold tightly to the hope we say we have, for God can be trusted to keep His promise" (Hebrews 10:23 NLT). He certainly can be trusted, so never lose hope.

2

Having Eyes to See

Having eyes, do you not see?

—MARK 8:18

In his novel *Until We Have Faces*, C.S. Lewis told the story of two sisters—Orual and Psyche, who were princesses happily living in the Kingdom of Glome. Everything in their lives was well until the priest of the goddess Ungit came to the king and told him that Psyche must be sacrificed to the goddess. Psyche is drugged and chained to the sacred tree, where she is left to be eaten by the Shadow-brute.

A few days later, Orual returns to the tree to give her sister's bones a proper burial. When she arrives, Psyche's bones are nowhere to be found. She wanders over to the river, crying, when she looks up to see Psyche standing on the other side. Orual is shocked. She doesn't know what to think. How is it possible? She knows that her sister is dead. How can this be true?

Orual crosses the river, she and Psyche embrace, and her sister tells her the story of how the god of the west wind saved her from the Shadow-brute. She describes how he has brought her to his palace to be his bride. Orual wonders whether she has lost her mind, but to humor her she listens to her sister's story as if she believes it.

Psyche leads Orual a short distance away to sit in the heather. There she serves her a glass of wine—the choicest of wine in an exquisite goblet. She asks Orual if she likes the goblet and the wine. Orual goes along with her and nods, but what she actually sees is her sister cupping her hands in a pool of water. Now she is sure Psyche has lost her mind.

Psyche goes on to tell Orual stories of gods and palaces and how she wears the most beautiful gowns. Orual sees no palace, only woods. No gowns, only her sister dressed in rags. After a while she can bear it no longer and demands that her sister show her the palace.

Orual is dumbfounded when her sister nods with a smile and says, "Of course I will. Let us go in."

Orual asks, "Is it far?"

"Far to where?" Psyche responds.

"To the palace," Orual shouts. "To your god's house!"

Psyche starts to tremble. "Orual, what do you mean, is it far?"

"Mean?" Orual asks. "Where is the palace? How far have we to go to reach it?"

Psyche starts to weep. Through her tears and cries, she stares into Orual's eyes and answers, "But this is it, Orual! Can't you see it? You are standing on the stairs to the great gate!"

Two people were in the same situation. One saw a palace. The other saw only the woods. One tasted expensive wine while the other tasted only muddy water. One saw a beautiful gown. The other saw rags. One saw great pillars at a palace entryway. The other saw only trees.

Orual was right on the steps of the palace, but she couldn't see it. Her perspective was skewed by a faulty paradigm. What Psyche saw was real, but Orual just didn't have eyes to see it.

What do you see in life? Do you have eyes to see what is real? To see Reality is simply to see through the eyes of faith. It means looking beyond the temporary aspect of this world and seeing the eternal. It means living by faith. Faith doesn't create anything—it simply sees what is already there. It looks beyond superficial senses and sees supernatural reality.

The apostle Paul described this kind of vision, saying, "We look not at the things which are seen, but at the things which are not seen; for the things which are seen are temporal, but the things which are not seen are eternal" (2 Corinthians 4:18).

As you move through your day, remember that what you see is only temporary. While the world around us is certainly real, it is not eternal.

You are an eternal being, and as such you can choose to not become a victim of superficial circumstances. This world is not your home. The Eternal defines who you are. Open your eyes and see it! Your destiny is to live with the King of kings in His palace. Hold that reality as the truth that can anchor you in the daily routine of life.

To become bogged down by things that are superficial can quickly cause you to be blinded to the things that are supernatural. While there are many things in this world whose urgency almost seems to capture your focus, it is possible to set your mind instead on the things that define you. Those are the love of God for you and your daily grace walk in the power of His Spirit. Choose to live intentionally within those realities, and don't let the flow of day-to-day frustrations cause you to become distracted from what really matters.

Choose to look beyond what can be perceived with natural senses and see the world that is really your home. As you perceive that world, everything in this life will be put into proper perspective.

3

A Busy Mind

You will keep in perfect peace
those whose minds are steadfast,
because they trust in you.

—ISAIAH 26:3 NIV

A too-busy mind can be a distraction from our daily grace walk. Some people can't even sleep well at night because of all the thoughts running through their heads. They're thinking about all that happened during the day; thinking about their plans for tomorrow; thinking about children, finances, past mistakes, future plans. Some even have imaginary conversations with people, picturing what they'll say if this happens or if that happens. Sometimes they even rehearse conversations of the day, thinking about what they *should* have said. Thinking, thinking, thinking!

Do you sometimes find yourself in a similar situation? It's not uncommon. Jesus even told His disciples on more than one occasion, "Take no thought." His instructions literally meant, "Don't take on the least bit of anxiety." Nothing drives away our sense of peace more than overthinking things. An overactive mind can keep you awake at night, leaving you tired during the day. It can prevent you from being able to stay focused on things that need your attention. It can cause you to start and then stop one project after another before you have completed them. It can cause you to wonder about your relationships with people, the security of your circumstances, the stability of your future…and it can certainly negatively affect how you perceive your relationship to God. The reason Jesus cautioned His disciples about anxiety is because He knows the extent to which a busy mind can weaken us in our grace walk.

It doesn't have to be that way. You aren't helpless over the thoughts that may bombard your mind. You might not be able to control what thought appears in your consciousness, but you can decide what you're going to do with it. The Bible tells us to bring every thought under the control of Christ. Paul wrote, "We are destroying speculations and every lofty thing raised up against the knowledge of God, and we are taking every thought captive to the obedience of Christ" (2 Corinthians 10:5). You don't have to be swept along by involuntary thoughts that flood your mind—instead, you can choose what to do with them as they come.

A busy mind can be the result of divided loyalties. In contrast, the more you understand how much God loves you and the more you learn to find contentment in that, the easier it will become to properly handle the thoughts that flood your mind. It is important to nurture yourself with the constant affirmation and realization of your Father's love and care in every area of life. Remember, anything that's important to you is important to Him.

Paul closed his letter to the Philippian church by instructing them about controlling their minds. He wrote, "Finally, brethren, whatever is true, whatever is honorable, whatever is right, whatever is pure, whatever is lovely, whatever is of good repute, if there is any excellence and if anything worthy of praise, dwell on these things" (Philippians 4:8). You can decide what you think about. You can direct your mind in such a way that peace will be your companion.

You can trust your way through your day or try to think your way through your day, but you'll soon learn that the first approach is far less stressful. Relentless reasoning about your circumstances is a way of trying to figure out how to control your own life independently. But we humans weren't created to live independently. Your Father's intent is that you learn to live in dependence on Him.

The mind must be brought in subjection to Him at each moment. It's not something you decide to do one time and then it is never a problem again. It is important to live each moment in surrender to Him. This isn't something that you have to consciously do. It can be the default you set for yourself each day.

That doesn't mean a barrage of thoughts won't ever rush in on you, disturbing your peace. While it may not be possible for you to silence thoughts that sometimes flood your mind, you can consciously submit the thoughts to your Father. As you grow in His grace and develop the habit of submitting a hyperactive mind to Him, He will bring growth to you. You will find rest while you learn more and more about continuously giving the details of life to Him.

There will always be outside influences that try to invade your thoughts and shift your focus away from Christ. When your mind runs wild, simply submit it all to Him. It's a choice you make. Some things in life you just aren't going to be able to think your way through—so you might as well save yourself the stress by simply *trusting* your way through them. Sure, we want answers now, but answers don't always come when we want. Learning that can bring tremendous peace to your life.

In Isaiah 26:3, the Bible says, "You will keep in perfect peace all who trust in you, all whose thoughts are fixed on you!" (NLT). The key to managing a barrage of thoughts is to set your mind on God. It is impossible to gaze into His loving face and be obsessed with the threats of your troubles at the same time. One glimpse into the face of the One who loves you more than you've ever been loved will reassure you that He superintends the details of your life.

The matter that is bringing you stress will most assuredly be resolved by your Father. Until that time comes, rest in His goodness and grace. Direct your mind to Him and to His goodness and love toward you. As you develop the habit of simple faith in His grace, you will experience peace. It is a peace that can come only when we keep our minds on Him.

4

A Job Well Done

God saw all that he had made, and it was very good.

—Genesis 1:31 NIV

It is a Godlike quality to be able to recognize a job well done. When God had created the heavens and the earth, He looked at His creation and affirmed that it was very good. What is your normal response when you complete a task? Do you look at it and find pleasure in the finished product? Or do you immediately notice all the ways—sometimes small, almost indistinguishable ways—that you could have done a better job? Your answer may say something about a perspective related to your faith.

After working on creation for six days, God rested on the seventh. He didn't rest because He was tired. He is all-powerful and never tires in the least. He rested because He was satisfied. The work was finished. His rest was one of fulfillment. It was the abiding peace of a job well done. God took pleasure in what He had done, and that quality is one He enjoys seeing in you.

There are different reasons people struggle with finding fulfillment in a job well done. Perfectionists seldom find a sense of satisfaction in anything they do. They nitpick themselves and their activities, picking everything to pieces. This is often rooted in an underlying sense of inadequacy that says, "I must do everything perfect to be okay." It's ironic that some people say, "I'm a perfectionist" almost as if they're bragging about it. Praying about it would make a lot more sense.

Perfectionism is not a virtue. It's often an indication that a person doesn't feel secure about their value unless what they do is beyond criticism. The problem is that the perfectionist is seldom able to see the "well done" of what they do because of insecurity. Perfectionism is an expression of an independent attitude that creates a sense of constant self-condemnation in those enslaved by it. If you see tendencies toward a perfectionist attitude within yourself, pray about it. Your Father wants to free you from constant self-judgment that refuses to applaud a job well done.

Other people can't recognize when they have done a good job because of a false sense of humility. Tell them they did well, and they'll dismiss your remark. They'll point out how they could have, should have, would have done better if things were different. False humility is, ironically, a form of pride. It is prideful because it causes a person to always focus on themselves and never be able to celebrate a finished task.

Do you find yourself shrugging off compliments for things you've done? If so, ask the Holy Spirit to teach you to respond in grace both inwardly and outwardly. The proper inward response to a compliment is satisfaction and gratitude. The outward response has to be no more complex than a simple "thank you," without further explanation or qualification.

God saw what He had done and said, "It is good." Some may argue, "But I'm not God!" That's true, but He is the One who is always at work in you to "will and to work for His good pleasure" (Philippians 2:13). The indwelling Christ is living and working through you—whether you're teaching a Bible study, working at your job, planting a flower garden, or cleaning out your garage. In whatever you do, there's really no such thing as secular activity, because Christ lives through you—all the time. He makes everything you do sacred because it's Him doing it in and through you.

To recognize and appreciate that you've done a good job is actually to affirm that He is the Source of your life and that He expresses Himself in the details of your daily life. Learn to celebrate a finished task and appreciate the value of what you've done. When you've done something good, see it as good!

In the Parable of the Talents, Jesus went so far as to indicate that when He returns and sees the faithful stewardship you've shown with those things He has entrusted to you, He might say, "Well done, good and faithful servant!" (Matthew 25:21 NIV). When He speaks those words to you, will you be able to receive them? If you find it hard to acknowledge an accomplishment now, maybe it would be a good idea to ask Him to begin to teach you to celebrate a job well done.

The proper response to a job you've done well will do two things: It will honor the One who has deposited within you the ability you possess, and it will help you cultivate a more positive attitude about yourself and what you do. Such an attitude is justified because your Father is proud of you. So don't insult Him by putting yourself or what you've done down. Rest in the fulfillment of a job well done and allow your mind to be renewed. This act will deepen your sense of peace and will bring glory to God.

5

Letting Go

*Whoever seeks to keep his life will lose it, and whoever loses
his life will preserve it.*

—Luke 17:33

Imagine a baby holding a pair of new shoes in his hands. He is playing with them, happy to have possession of them. His parent reaches down to take the shoes and put them on the child's feet. All the child sees is that his shoes are being taken out of his hands. He doesn't like it. He's fascinated by them and wants to be in control of them and keep them in his hands. That's how babies are.

The baby begins to cry. He is overwhelmed with anger, confusion, and regret that his shoes are being taken away. He screams. He kicks in protest. He is losing control of the thing he loves and wants to hold. He doesn't understand what his parent is doing, but the parent does understand and does what is necessary. Shoes aren't made to be toys. Their purpose is to be worn and walked in.

The goal is to enable the child to enjoy the shoes to the fullest by experiencing their intended purpose. The parent knows that if the shoes are used for their designed purpose, the child will truly benefit and not simply be amused by them.

We can all act like babies at times. The urge to be in control of our own lives is something that rises up in every believer throughout life. The irony of it is that we weren't created to be in control, at least not all by ourselves. The divine purpose is that we live our lives under God's control and that we take charge of the things that affect us in this life by depending on Him as our life source.

You may feel like there are circumstances in your life that are out of control, but they aren't. They are simply out of *your* control. Your life is in God's hands, and everything is under *His* control.

What is it in your life that you need to release? It might be control over your finances, your reputation, your spouse, your children, your future, something else from among countless other things. When we try to hold onto something and refuse to relinquish it and put it into God's hands, we are depriving ourselves of His best plan for our lives. Maybe your loving Father wants to bless you in a greater way—a new way—but the only way He may be able to do that is if you are willing to release your grip on what you're trying to hold right now.

Only a baby thinks the highest pleasure is to hold what is his in his hands. He doesn't see the whole picture. So the parent overrules the child's wishes, takes the shoes, for instance, and does what is needful. Eventually the child will understand. When he does, he is thrilled, and more important than that, he walks.

Do you want to make real progress in your grace walk? Let go of what you are holding onto right now. Whatever you hold and try to control will ultimately control you. What appears to be loss from your perspective may actually be your loving Father taking something out of your control so He can do what He wants to do with it and with you.

Plato was once walking down a road and saw a man's cattle in his field. He noted that the cows could go wherever they wanted and do whatever they wanted within that field. The man, on the other hand, couldn't be gone for long because he had to be home to feed the cattle. Did the man own the cattle? Plato wondered. Or did the cattle own the man?

To insist that your possessions are rightfully yours may not be the best course to take. Instead, hold on to the possessions, people, and circumstances you find yourself with lightly, knowing that your Father always has your best interest at heart.

There may have been times in your life when it seemed that something was taken away. You didn't like the way things happened when they happened, but in time you came to see that it really was the best thing. That's always the case, whether we see it or not. Without the eternal vantage point, it's impossible for us to see that we aren't losing anything, but the situation is actually the hand of our Father doing what needs to be done so that we can walk the wonderful course He has planned for us.

Whatever you find in your hands today, hold onto it loosely. Claim no personal ownership over it but recognize that you are simply a steward of it. Your God may leave it in your hands, or He may not. Either way, it's under His control. If He should take it out of your hand, remember who He is and who you are—and trust Him with it.

6

Childlike Faith

*Truly I say to you, unless you are converted and become
like children, you will not enter the kingdom of heaven.*

—Matthew 18:3

The five-year-old girl stood on the windowsill, leaning against the glass
with her arms stretched out, wearing the kind of smile that is so big it
only fits a child. Outside, the rain was pounding, the thunder was explod-
ing, and the lightning flashed again and again.

The little girl's daddy walked past the door, glanced in, and saw her.
Rushing to the window, he asked, "What are you doing?" His daughter
pointed to the flashes of lightning outside. "I think God is trying to take
my picture," she answered.

Here was a little girl who understood her heavenly Father's heart. Do
you understand His heart toward you like this child did? Your *Abba* is
proud of you. The Bible says that in the ages to come, you will show forth
the exceeding riches of His grace. Your life is an eternal picture of God's
pride in those He loves.

When my granddaughter was a six-year-old, I asked her the question, "Do you know how beautiful you are?" Without hesitation, she
answered, "Yes." Some might say her answer reflected the seed of pride. I
say it reflected a simple trust in what those she loves have told her. She has
been showered with love her whole life. She has been told that she is precious and beautiful, and she has simply believed it.

Jesus said, "Truly I say to you, unless you are converted and become like children, you will not enter the kingdom of heaven" (Matthew 18:3). Many adults need a conversion. They need to be converted from the analytical assessments of an adult to the simple faith of a child. According to Jesus, that's the only way we will enter the kingdom of God.

Have you retained childlike trust in your God? Are you secure in His love for you? Do you really believe how much He treasures you? The self-perception of some people has been tainted by negative input from others. Employers, spouses, parents, friends, and even clergy have caused them to question their true value. Have you made the mistake of allowing criticism and demeaning messages—direct or indirect—to cause you to lose sight of your true value? You don't have to spend a lifetime focusing on shortcomings you perceive in yourself. Your Creator is a God of grace, and what He sees is the beauty in you.

Will you choose to believe what your Father says about you? Ephesians 2:10 says, "We are His workmanship, created in Christ Jesus for good works, which God prepared beforehand so that we would walk in them." The Greek word translated here as *workmanship* could as easily be rendered *poem*. You are a divine work of art!

Your Father says that He rejoices over you with an enthusiasm that causes Him to sing and dance. One Bible version paraphrases Zephaniah 3:17 like this:

> The LORD your God has arrived to live among you. He is a
> mighty savior. He will rejoice over you with great gladness.
> With his love, he will calm all your fears. He will exult over
> you by singing a happy song (NLT).

God's opinion of you is the final word on the subject. Don't argue about your worth with the One who created you. Your value is a gift to you through Jesus Christ. His love for you has bestowed upon you a value that is breathtaking when you come to see it. Understand and believe that God adores you and it will change the way you look at yourself and your life. After all, "if God is for us, who can be against us?" (Romans 8:31 NIV).

Will you believe the truth of your Father's absolute adoration of you? A study of the life of the nation of Israel in the Old Testament shows that its behavior was inconsistent at best. Its obedience and faith waxed and waned throughout God's dealings with her. To His glory, His grace continued to abound toward the nation despite its instable actions. In Isaiah 43:4, He said, "You are precious in My sight." He goes on to say, "You are honored and I love you."

That is the declaration of God in the Old Testament toward His people, who had been disobedient again and again! Do you think that His affection and esteem for you is any less? Don't let an adult perspective interfere with your faith in Him and His love for you.

Cast off the cancerous cynicism of a jaded adult and embrace the simple faith of a child. Your *Abba* loves and adores you. If *that* is true, then everything else we face in this world is small by comparison. Ask your Father to help you mature in grace until you reach the place of the simple faith of a child. Believe the truth about yourself because the One who brought you into existence has said it is so. You are your heavenly Father's child. You really are a beautiful child of God. To believe that isn't prideful, because you've done nothing to make yourself become that way. He has done it all. So just thank Him and then walk in childlike confidence based on what He has told you about yourself.

Christ, Our Anchor

*This hope we have as an anchor of the soul,
a hope both sure and steadfast and one
which enters within the veil.*

—Hebrews 6:19

Some years ago, my wife, Melanie, and I were on a sailing trip alone. We reached a small island where we wanted to spend the night. Normally we would pick up a mooring ball, where we would tie off our boat to secure it for the night. These mooring balls are set in concrete and are securely anchored at the bottom of the ocean. When a boat is tied off to one of them, nothing can move it.

It was late enough in the day that we couldn't find a mooring ball because too many other boats had arrived ahead of us. Because of the hour I was hesitant to set sail to another place to spend the night, so we decided to set anchor where we were. In the few years we had been sailing, we hadn't gained confidence that we were able to successfully set the anchor so it would hold firmly through the night. We had been taught how to do it when we had taken sailing certification classes, but we were still unsure.

My fears caused me to imagine what would happen if the anchor pulled loose during the middle of the night. We could drift and bump into other boats around us. I wasn't worried so much about doing damage to our or another boat—rather, I didn't want to look like I didn't know what I was doing (which wasn't totally without truth). Another possibility was that we might drift from where we were to the water's edge and find ourselves on the nearby reef. Or I imagined we could even wake up the next morning with the boat adrift out in the middle of the channel.

We set the anchor. Then I sat in one spot on deck, lining up a point on the boat with an object on land to make sure we weren't drifting. Everything appeared to be okay, but I still wasn't easy about it. We took our dinghy ashore to have dinner, but throughout the whole meal I kept watching to make sure our boat was still in the same place.

That night when we went below to sleep, I jerked awake almost every time I felt any movement that seemed unusual. I even got up and went up on deck four or five times during the night and checked the anchor to make sure it was still secure. It was a long night with only brief moments of sleep.

When the sun came up the next day, I checked the anchor again. It hadn't moved at all. Everything had been fine. My fears and apprehension had been unfounded.

I thought about that experience later and began to see how much that experience reflected my attitude in life at times. There we were in a beautiful island setting, but I didn't really enjoy it that evening or night. I can't even remember what I ate at the restaurant where we had dinner. I don't remember the sunset that evening. I didn't enjoy the gentle sway of the boat in the water rocking me to sleep, which I normally would. I was too worried, too focused on what might happen if the anchor didn't hold.

Hebrews 6:19 assures us that our hope in Christ is an "anchor of the soul." Despite that promise, there have been times in my life when I couldn't fully enjoy being where God had put me at the time because of fears—fears of drifting out of His will, fears about dangers I thought I could see on the horizon, fears about looking like I didn't know what I was doing. Fear robs us of the joy of the journey known as "life." It causes us to believe that our safety is up to us, not God. It makes us act like we are the ones who have to make sure everything turns out well.

Are you going through anything in your life right now that causes you to be afraid about what might happen? We all do at times, but the key to successfully dealing with those times in life isn't to hope that they don't happen or that our situation will lead to a good outcome. The key is in learning to let it go and to entrust ourselves and life's circumstances to the One who has it all under control.

8

Cling to Jesus

*The people remained at a distance, while Moses
approached the thick darkness where God was.*

—Exodus 20:21 niv

When God was ready to interact with Moses on Mount Sinai, Moses had to walk directly into the darkness—"thick darkness" the Bible calls it. But there was an amazing thing about it. It was in that thick darkness that he would meet God and hear Him speak directly. Sometimes the darkness is where we are most likely to see and hear God.

A big misconception many people have is that if we can just find the right biblical formula and follow it, things will turn out the way we want. Modern Christianity often suggests that to follow Christ means that, as long as we're doing the things we've been told we're supposed to do, we can expect sunshine in the circumstances of our lives. Then life's situations step into plain view, and we realize it's not working the way we've believed it would.

When we believe we can ensure a particular result from God by what we do for Him, we are treating Him like a divine vending machine. If we put the right things in, the things we want will come out in life. Experience soon shows that neither He nor life is a vending machine, with which a certain payment automatically produces a certain product.

Have you felt like the things you've learned about how a certain kind of behavior will always produce a particular outcome just aren't true? Have you been disappointed because you've felt you've done all the right things and the result hasn't been what you thought it would be or *should* be?

The reality is that neither biblical faith nor our God works that way. Our Father is good, but we can't manipulate Him or situations in life by doing A and expecting B. Sometimes there's a fine line between honoring God through our actions and subtly trying to get what we want from Him by turning our actions into a formula we expect to yield a certain result. The grace walk isn't built around formulas—it is grounded in faith in the loving-kindness of the One whose we are.

What are we to do when our situations don't unfold in the way we were sure they would after we've done all the right things? What do we do when we see nothing but a thick, dark cloud where we had anticipated a bright day? When we can't make sense of how things have turned out, what is the answer? It's this: Walk in the darkness and cling to Jesus.

When you have made a serious decision in faith and things have still gone sour, cling to Jesus. When you read your Bible but don't seem to get anything out of it at all, cling to Jesus. When your bills are coming in faster than your paychecks do, cling to Jesus. When your children make decisions that contradict everything you've taught them their whole lives, cling to Jesus. When the doctor gives the diagnosis you most feared to hear, cling to Jesus. When you aren't sure which minister is teaching truth and which is teaching error, cling to Jesus. When grace is something you believe, but you wonder how to move it from your head to your experience, cling to Jesus. When your heart has grown cold and you haven't felt God's presence in a very long time, cling to Jesus. When a friend betrays you in a way you never would have imagined, cling to Jesus.

Cling to Jesus. He will guide you through His Spirit. He will nurture you by His love. He will provide for you through His generosity. He will comfort you through His tender compassion. He will heal you by His stripes. He will reveal truth to you through the Scriptures. He will transform you by His power. He will touch you by His presence. He will sustain you by His faithfulness.

Cling to Jesus. He holds you in His arms at this very moment and will never let you go. You have been bought with a price, and you will display the glory of His grace throughout eternity. Cling to Jesus and know this for sure—He will eternally cling to you. You may be in the dark, but He will never let go.

9

Dead Pods and New Life

I am the vine, you are the branches; he who
abides in Me and I in him, he bears much fruit,
for apart from Me you can do nothing.

—John 15:5

That crape myrtle tree is going to look terrible all season," I commented to my wife, Melanie, one day as we left the house. The tree is right outside our front door. I had kept intending to prune it during the winter, but neglected the job all season. A few days earlier I had noticed the beginning of new, green growth on the tree. But the old, ugly, dead pods from last year were still clinging to the limbs.

Later that month as we backed out of our driveway, I noticed the tree again. In a few short weeks, an amazing transformation had taken place. Most of the dead pods were gone, lying on the ground beneath its limbs. New growth now filled most of the tree, reaching out to the tips of the branches where blossoms would soon appear.

As I looked at the transformation that had occurred, the thought came to me: *That's exactly what happens in the life of those who trust in Christ!* We have His life, but at times the old wrong behavioral patterns are still clinging to us. They are ugly and obviously dead, but they are there nonetheless.

What are we to do when we see ugly remnants of a past season of our lives still hanging on? The common legalistic approach involves putting forth serious effort to rid ourselves of those ugly sins that won't let go.

Many people have been made to believe that the problem is simply that they aren't trying hard enough or trusting sincerely enough to experience victory. Or worse yet, they've been taught that it's up to them to prune away all the dead growth they still see. That kind of teaching is far removed from the grace of God.

Depending on your religious tradition, you may have been told to read your Bible more, to pray more, to memorize Scripture, to fast, to verbally renounce the sins, to cast out devils, to see a Christian counselor. The only answer empty religion can offer is yet another prescription for moral behavior modification. The problem is that it never works. Only Jesus works.

As we yield ourselves to Him and focus our attention on Him and not on our sins, His life rises up in us and changes everything. What religious determination can't do, Jesus can do. When our effort fails, His life can prevail!

Have you found that to be true in your life? Grace offers good news when we find ourselves in the place where we know there is nothing left we can do to successfully get rid of sins. As you grow in grace, a transformation takes place in your life. The life of Christ surging through you will begin to fill you to such an extent that the old behavior will begin to drop away. The ugly remnants of a season gone by will be eliminated one by one as New Life fills you. You don't have to prune away the sins of your lifestyle. Instead, just look to Jesus and trust Him to transform your lifestyle!

Jesus said, "I am the vine, you are the branches." That verse offers real hope. As we trust in Him, we will discover that it isn't necessary to try to prune our own life of the ugly things that still are holding onto us. Legalistic religion will tell you that it is up to you to do away with the dead deeds of your lifestyle, but the reality is that you don't have the ability to do that. He will do it for you.

Simply depend on Him and you'll experience a real expression of grace. You will be overjoyed to see that when you truly know you are rooted and grounded in the love of the Father, the remnants of the old life will lose their grip and fall away. Ultimately, His life will fill the branches of your behavior. And it will have happened without a struggle on your part.

As surely as the seasons change, our heavenly Father will finish the job

He has started in you. You have been predestined to be conformed to the image of His Son. Romans 8:29 says,

> God knew what he was doing from the very beginning. He decided from the outset to shape the lives of those who love him along the same lines as the life of his Son. The Son stands first in the line of humanity he restored. We see the original and intended shape of our lives there in him (MSG).

Nothing, not even dead pods from a nasty old lifestyle, will stop His work in you. God always finishes what He starts. First Thessalonians 5:24 says, "Faithful is He who calls you, and He also will bring it to pass."

Do you see ugly things that are still in your life? Let your roots grow deep in His grace and watch the transformation. His grace really is sufficient! New life will replace dead pods of yesterday's bad behavior. You will experience the grace walk as you trust Him, not as you try harder.

Don't Touch the Cactus

*Jesus said, "I do not condemn you, either.
Go. From now on sin no more."*

—JOHN 8:11

The cactuses were covered with flowers, a sight not often seen by the five-year-old boy from the East Coast. "Don't touch the cactus," his mother told him as he reached out to pick the flower. "It will hurt you," she went on to explain.

But as often happens with small children, the mother had no sooner turned her back for a moment than she heard a young voice give a pain-filled cry. Turning around, she saw that her child had done exactly what she had just told him not to do. He was now running toward her with his index finger held high in the air while he squeezed it with the other hand. "It hurts, Mommy!" he cried. "It hurts!"

Quickly the loving mother picked the child up in her arms. "That's why I told you not to touch it. Here, let's see. Don't cry. Mommy will take the prickly needle out of your finger."

Did you know that the Bible compares the love of God to that of a mother? Isaiah 49:15 asks, "Can a mother...have no compassion on the child she has borne?" (NIV). It's just not possible, no matter what the child does. Even in his disobedience, a mother's first concern is for the welfare of the one she gave birth to. Nothing can ever change that.

"I will *never*...forsake you," promises the God who gave birth to you

(Hebrews 13:5). Nothing you have ever done or ever will do can cause God to abandon you. He loves you. He *loves* you. That fact will never change. When we learn to rest in that reality, we will respond rightly when we've sinned.

What was the first thing Adam and Eve did after they sinned? They hid from God. Genesis 3:9-10 says, "The Lord God called to the man, and said to him, 'Where are you?' He said, 'I heard the sound of You in the garden, and I was afraid because I was naked; so I hid myself.'" Sin has always caused people to become blind to the Light of Grace and to hide, but that certainly doesn't need to be our response.

Jesus Christ doesn't stand ready to condemn or even judge you when you've sinned. Consider how he treated the woman caught committing adultery (John 8). The religious world stood ready to convict, condemn, and execute her. The gracious response of Jesus to her situation was (and still is) completely out of sync with the religious mindset. "God did not send his Son into the world to condemn the world, but to save the world through him" (John 3:17 NIV).

Jesus didn't come to bring revenge, but restoration and reconciliation between humanity and God. Others may condemn you for your sins. You may condemn yourself for them, but Jesus Christ brings no judgment against you in the slightest.

Does He care when we sin? Of course He does, but not for the reason you may think. On the cross He defeated sin and "put away sin by the sacrifice of Himself" (Hebrews 9:25-26). Sin poses no threat to God. He is not a hypersanitary deity who refuses to come close to you when you've sinned lest He be contaminated by it.

To the contrary, He has become sin for you so that you might become the righteousness of God in Him (2 Corinthians 5:21). The reason Jesus hates to see you sin is because of what it does to you, not to Him. Sin wrecks and ravages a person's life, as evidenced by the woman caught in adultery.

Jesus told the woman that He didn't condemn her. He doesn't condemn you either. He told her to go and not keep committing the sin of adultery because He loved her and didn't want to see her life be wrecked by that sin. That's His concern with your sin too. It isn't about morality. It never has been. What is important to Him is that you be free from sins and don't touch those things that hurt you, because He doesn't want you to be hurt!

As with the small child with the prickly cactus needle in his finger, our sins should drive us *toward* God, not away. Your sins don't define who you are. They may attach themselves *to* you when you disobey, but they aren't *you*.

So, when you've sinned, don't run and hide. Instead run toward God and you'll discover Him running toward you. Don't try to hide your sin. Hold it up for Him to see, and cry out, "It hurts! It hurts!" He won't scold you for your disobedience. You won't be given a lecture about your foolish behavior.

Instead, you will be held and gently set free from the pain you've brought on yourself. Then you'll be lovingly hugged and tenderly told, "Now, go play. And don't touch the cactus again." ("Go, and sin no more.")

11

A Friendly Universe

This I know, that God is for me.

—Psalm 56:9

Someone once asked Albert Einstein, "Of all the questions you've posed about the mysteries of the universe, which question do you think is the most important?" Einstein's response: "Is the universe a friendly place or not?" That is an important question, and the answer isn't hard to know. Our Creator is a friendly God, and He is sovereign over the universe. So wherever we are, we can trust Him to work all things together for our good.

Is the universe friendly? It doesn't matter. The God who rules the universe is definitely friendly. That fact is enough to equip you to navigate through anything life seems to throw at you.

Speaking to His disciples shortly before His crucifixion, Jesus said, "I no longer call you servants, because a servant does not know his master's business. Instead, I have called you friends, for everything that I learned from my Father I have made known to you" (John 15:15 NIV). There's the big difference between empty religion and an exciting relationship with Christ!

A legalistic, religious viewpoint will cause you to see God purely as the One who has expectations of you that you'll never be able to successfully meet. Of course there is a sense in which we are servants of God, but it's not the kind of servant who must obey and serve in order to be accepted. We serve out of the overflow of pleasure we experience from walking arm in arm with our dear Friend each moment.

Your God is for you, and to the extent that you clearly understand that reality, you'll find yourself being motivated to live boldly, knowing that your very existence brings honor to Him. His delight is in you, not in what you do. On the other hand, grace instills in us a desire to live in a way that honors Him. Just as it brings us joy to bring pleasure to other friends, we find joy in bringing pleasure to our Father. Knowing that God is for you will free you from self-consciousness about any shortcomings that you may perceive yourself to have. When you accept His complete acceptance of you as His friend, everything changes.

How you think about life is very important. Your mindset is like a thermostat for the temperature of your attitude. Your attitude will ultimately determine your feelings, and feelings have great potential to influence actions. That's why this matter of properly understanding our Father's mind toward us is so important.

God is for you—so don't anticipate bad things, because a good God has your best interest at heart. Painful situations will sometimes arise, but even in the dark times, His loving faithfulness and strength is there to support you. As you look forward, make it your habit to assume God's underlying goodness in every situation you face in life. Knowing that He is for you enables you to set a course for your life based on the truth.

It was David the psalmist who wrote, "This I know, that God is for me," and like all of us, David experienced the ups and downs of life. But his faith remained steadfast. Without absolute confidence that God is on your side, circumstances may toss your emotions around like a cork in the ocean. However, the person who has settled on the fact of God's goodness is able to calmly move forward in anticipation of a good outcome.

Does that mean that we always get what we want? Not at all, but it does mean that while our path may be a winding one that sometimes leads us through dark valleys, all the while we are progressing toward a good place. Anyplace God leads us is a good place because it is His place for our lives, and He is there with us.

The apostle Paul described it with poetic beauty:

> I am convinced that nothing can ever separate us from his love.
> Death can't, and life can't. The angels can't, and the demons
> can't. Our fears for today, our worries about tomorrow, and even

the powers of hell can't keep God's love away. Whether we are high above the sky or in the deepest ocean, nothing in all creation will ever be able to separate us from the love of God that is revealed in Christ Jesus our Lord (Romans 8:38-39 NLT).

With that biblical assurance as your foundation, you have every reason to expect the best. Consider every positive result in your life to be a reminder from God of His intent to bless you. When painful things happen, be assured that He is with you and that "this too shall pass." Look for His hand and listen for His voice in the small things of your day. Your God is a good God, and He has already worked out the details for your life. He stands tall over the past, present, and future. He was with you in your past. He is with you now, and He is waiting in your future for you to catch up and see the wonderful things He has planned for you!

See the goodness of God in this day. Cultivate the habit of recognizing that the Source of every good thing that comes your way is a loving Father who is for you and wants to bless you. Don't miss His daily expressions of love by failing to see the evidence that He is for you in the little things that work to your favor. Good things that may seem incidental aren't. They are the whisper of a God who gently says, "See, I am for you."

12

Looking for a Revival

*I pray that your hearts will be flooded with light so that you can
understand the confident hope he has given to those he called—
his holy people who are his rich and glorious inheritance.*

—Ephesians 1:18 nlt 2004

Public opinion in the church world today is that we are in need of a
revival. Are you one who thinks that the need in your spiritual life is to
experience a personal revival? It might surprise you to know that a revival
is not what you really need. It's not what any of us need.

The church tradition of my early life often included "revival services,"
a series of worship services that usually lasted a week. The meetings usually included zealous singing followed by a fiery evangelist sharing a sermon that moved many of us to rededicate our lives to Christ. We would
be admonished to repent of our sinful or slothful ways and promise God
that, with His help, we would do better.

Actually, these revivals often felt invigorating and motivating, but the
big problem was that they weren't self-perpetuating. We had to schedule
revival meetings twice a year at church because, as surely as the autumn
leaves would fall, our spring revival would have worn off and we would
need to do it all over again. We didn't mind, though, because it felt so good
to "get right with God" and start afresh and anew.

It isn't my intent to scoff at the tradition of my childhood or yours if
you share it. We were all sincere, and our scheduled revival services came

from a noble desire to please God. As a pastor, I carried the tradition forward for many years in the churches I served, but like many things I did as a legalist, my efforts were misguided.

The word *revival* isn't even found in the New Testament, but more important, neither is the concept. Revival is an Old Covenant experience. Once the New Covenant became effective, we received something better—*resurrection*. We have been resurrected to a new life in Christ. Understanding our life in Christ is the only catalyst for a godly lifestyle that endures.

The apostle Paul never prayed for revival in the church, but instead prayed for the revelation of the meaning of the love of God and what it means to walk in His power. Here's how he said it:

> I keep asking that the God of our Lord Jesus Christ, the glorious Father, may give you the Spirit of wisdom and revelation, so that you may know him better. I pray that the eyes of your heart may be enlightened in order that you may know the hope to which he has called you, the riches of his glorious inheritance in his holy people, and his incomparably great power for us who believe (Ephesians 1:17-19 NIV).

Paul said, "I'm praying for you to have the Spirit of wisdom and revelation so that you may *know*." The need isn't to have our religious batteries recharged or our spiritual fuel tank refilled. That's Old Testament thinking. It's a new day—a day of grace. The only thing we need now is to know Him—to have our eyes opened so that we will understand all that is our birthright in Jesus Christ.

So this whole revival idea is yesterday's news from an old covenant that has been made obsolete. The news today is that our loving God wants us to experience a revelation of who He is in us and who we are in Him. Understanding His unconditional love and unwavering grace brings something so much greater than revival. It brings Spirit-produced reformation of our lives. It restructures our understanding of what it means to be in Christ and reorders the way we live. It causes us to give up on the silly notion that we can live up to the promises we make when we rededicate ourselves to God during a church meeting. A revelation of our identity in

Christ brings us to the place of total dependence on Him, understanding that it is only by His grace that we will ever be able to live a lifestyle that truly honors Him.

Revival happens when we make heartfelt promises to do better. Righteous reformation happens in our lives when we depend on Jesus within us to be who He is through us. Revival is short-lived. The revelation of the resurrected life brought to us by Him is permanent. Revival is taught in the Old Testament. Revelation of Jesus Christ is the message of the New Covenant. Revival produces motivation. Spirit-produced reformation produces genuine transformation.

What we need is a reformation that comes through the revelation of grace. Grace in your life is the divine enablement for you to be all that you have been called to be and do all that you have been called to do. It isn't about your dedication to Him.

It's time to stop praying for revival. Instead, pray for a revelation of Christ in you in such a way that you increasingly see more and more of your true identity in Him. That revelation will produce a transformation in you that won't need to be repeated again and again.

13

Watering Down the Gospel

I do not nullify the grace of God, for if righteousness comes through the Law, then Christ died needlessly.

—GALATIANS 2:21

Many devotional books tell people that they need to do better so they can become a better person. This one won't tell you that for one simple reason: The word *gospel* means "good news," and nothing could be further from good news than being told you're expected to muster up more self-effort to try harder to do better. If you're like most of us, you've probably tried that approach many times and have seen that it just doesn't work for long. The fact is that there's only one way to live the life that belongs to you through Christ. We live it the same way we received it—by faith.

Paul wrote to the believers in Galatia about this very thing. The people in the Galatian church had trusted Christ when Paul taught them the gospel, but after he left there, things jumped track. A group of false teachers had come into the church telling them that, while they were indeed on their way to heaven, they had a personal responsibility to keep certain religious rules in the meantime. Their part, said these legalists, began by being circumcised, which would be an indication of their intent to keep a whole list of religious rules about to be imposed on them.

Paul wrote and actually called them "idiots" for falling for such foolishness. The God's Word translation renders it this way: "You stupid people of Galatia! Who put you under an evil spell? Wasn't Christ Jesus' crucifixion clearly described to you?" Harsh words, but it was a very important subject. The future of their grace walk was in jeopardy.

Paul was asking them, "Have you had some sort of spell cast on you? You became a Christian without doing a single thing, but now you think that what you do is an important part of growing in your life in Christ? Did you become a Christian by anything you did or didn't do? No? Then what makes you think that now you are a Christian, what you do has anything at all to do with receiving God's blessings? Does God work in and among you because of what you do or because you simply trust Him?"

Paul knew that, in this instance, direct and even harsh words were necessary. The gospel is the fantastic news that you and I have been made righteous because of what Christ has done, not because of what we do. In fact, there's nothing for you to do—just believe it! For anybody to say that there is something you must do before *or after* starting to follow Jesus so that you can become more righteous is to water down the pure gospel of Jesus Christ and to insult what He accomplished at the cross. The righteousness of God is a gift, not a goal we have in life (Romans 5:17).

To think that you can become more righteous by doing "all the right things" is to act as if God's grace doesn't exist. Paul wrote, ""I do not nullify the grace of God, for if righteousness comes through the Law, then Christ died needlessly" (Galatians 2:21). He was saying that if righteousness can be gained by keeping religious rules there was no point in Jesus' going to the cross. To suggest that religious rule-keeping has anything to do with a grace walk is to nullify the grace of God.

When Paul realized the Galatians were about to get caught up in religious rules, here's what he wrote them:

> Let me put this question to you: How did your new life begin? Was it by working your heads off to please God? Or was it by responding to God's Message to you? Are you going to continue this craziness? For only crazy people would think they could complete by their own efforts what was begun by God. If you weren't smart enough or strong enough to begin it, how do you suppose you could perfect it? (Galatians 3:2-3 MSG).

The next time you hear anybody saying that there is something you need to do to become more righteous, I hope an alarm goes off in your mind. That's not grace. Not everybody who says they believe the Bible has this matter straight in their own minds. If they tell you that you should keep certain rules, they may be sincere but they are sincerely wrong! Legalism is very subtle at times. Remember that a diluted gospel is a polluted gospel, which is no gospel (good news) at all. Don't fall for a watered-down gospel, such as that being taught by many today.

The gospel is the good news that you are 100 percent righteous because of what *He* has done, not because of anything you need to do. You don't have to do anything. Ironically, once you understand that fact, you will find that you *want* to do some things, but it won't be because you've bought into guilty manipulation that has nothing to do with the true message of the gospel. It will be because you are motivated by the loving grace of God.

14

Does Grace Encourage Sin?

*Sin shall not be master over you, for you
are not under law but under grace.*

—ROMANS 6:14

The message of grace is scandalous to the religious mind. The idea that people can get off scot-free for the wrong things they've done galls the self-righteous. This kind of thinking causes some to think that grace will weaken people's dedication to Christ and cause them to not take sin seriously. Grace scares some people. "Give them an inch and they'll take a mile." The fear is that pure grace is dangerous. After all, if people get the idea that all their sins have been completely put away, won't that encourage them to misbehave?

Not according to Jesus. Luke 7:36-50 teaches the truth about the power of complete forgiveness. Jesus is eating in the home of a Pharisee, when a woman known to have a bad reputation comes to Him. She brings a box of perfume and, as she weeps, takes her hair and washes His feet with the perfume.

The Pharisee sees this and thinks to himself, *If Jesus were really a man of God, he would know what kind of woman this is and wouldn't allow it.*

Knowing what the man was thinking, Jesus said to him, "A moneylender had two debtors. One owed him ten times as much as the other. Neither could repay him, so the man forgave them both. Which of them will love him more?"

"The one whom he forgave the most," the man answered.

"You are exactly right," Jesus said, "and the same is true of this woman. I entered your house and you didn't wash my feet, but she has washed my feet with tears and wiped them with her hair. You haven't kissed me once, but she hasn't stopped kissing my feet."

Then Jesus answered this Pharisee and every other person who thinks that grace encourages sin. He said, "For this reason I say to you, her sins, which are many, have been forgiven, for she loved much; but he who is forgiven little, loves little" (verse 47). What caused this woman to love Jesus much? It was the realization of how much she had been forgiven.

The greater the forgiveness, the greater the love. That's what Jesus said. So to teach people that all the sins of their lifetime have been forgiven will not cause them to sin. It will cause them to love Jesus more! We don't have to be afraid that grace encourages sin, because it doesn't.

Titus 2:11-12 says, "The grace of God has appeared, bringing salvation to all men, instructing us to deny ungodliness and worldly desires and to live sensibly, righteously and godly in the present age." The only ones who think grace leads to sin are those who don't understand what grace really does in a person's life.

The sins of your whole lifetime have been forgiven. Paul wrote in Colossians 2:13-14,

> When you were dead in your transgressions and the uncircumcision of your flesh, He made you alive together with Him, having forgiven us all our transgressions, having canceled out the certificate of debt consisting of decrees against us, which was hostile to us; and He has taken it out of the way, having nailed it to the cross.

The sins of your entire lifetime were dealt with at the cross. Old Covenant Law rendered you guilty, but the charges against you have been dropped for lack of evidence. Not only has Jesus taken away your sins as if they never happened, He has also delivered you from the place where those laws that condemned you had any authority over you!

God's grace is so big that it has both destroyed your sins and taken you out of the world of law where the basis for your guilt existed. This idea is almost too good for some to accept, but it's true. *All* your sins are gone.

The idea that the sins we haven't even committed yet have been forgiven is an offense to some people because they're scared it will encourage a careless lifestyle. But that isn't what the Bible teaches. As Jesus taught, the greater our understanding of forgiveness, the greater the love.

The obstacle that most people have trouble getting past in accepting the reality that all their sins have been forgiven is the idea that future sins could already be dealt with even before we commit them. I remind you, though, that when Christ died for our sins, He died for *all* of them—and we hadn't even been born yet. If Christ could take every sin we would commit upon Himself at the cross before we had committed a single one of them, why couldn't He forgive them in the same way?

He can and He did. Your sins are forgiven. Not just some of them, but all of them.

Now, what *if* every sin of your lifetime is already forgiven? What difference would that make in how you live from day to day? I can tell you the difference: It would free you to take your eyes off yourself and put them on Christ and on others. It would deliver you from self-consciousness and sin-consciousness.

The fact is, your sins *have* all been forgiven. That won't cause you or anybody else to run wild. The apostle Paul answered that objection when he asked, "If all this about grace is true, does that mean we just sin like crazy because we know it's all covered by grace?" He answered his own question: "God forbid! How can we live in sin if we have already died to it? Or don't you understand that every one of us who have been placed into Jesus Christ were with Him when He died? The reality is that when somebody dies, they are free from sin—and we died!" (paraphrased from Romans 6:1-7).

You can relax about the fear that grace will cause people to sin. It won't. Instead, it will cause those who understand the scope of forgiveness to love Jesus more, take their eyes off themselves, and live freely. Starting today, try it in your own life and you'll see the proof.

15

Looking in the Wrong Places

*Listen to me, you who pursue righteousness, who seek
the LORD: Look to the rock from which you were
hewn and to the quarry from which you were dug.*

—ISAIAH 51:1

One day, as I was about to leave our home, I picked up my keys and my money clip from the table beside my chair in the living room. My sunglasses weren't there. I went to my desk in my home office, and they weren't there either. "Have you seen my sunglasses?" I called out to my wife, Melanie, who was in the other room. "No, I haven't seen them," she answered.

I always keep my sunglasses on the table beside my chair. So I went back into the living room and looked again. No, they weren't there. So back to my desk I went to look more carefully. (This is a ridiculous habit I have, looking in the same places more than once when I've lost something.) The glasses still weren't there.

"Are you sure you didn't move them when you were cleaning?" I yelled to Melanie again. "I haven't touched them," she answered. *Maybe I left them beside the bed on the nightstand,* I thought. But they weren't there either.

Now I was beginning to get frustrated. I knew that my sunglasses hadn't just disappeared, and I knew that Melanie had cleaned the living room earlier in the day. It doesn't take a genius (Just a husband) to put two and two together. "Melanie," I called, "you must have moved them. They aren't where

I left them." "I *haven't* touched your glasses," she said from the other room in a way that let me know I was pushing the envelope. *Why in the world would she move them and then not remember?* I silently thought to myself.

Then the thought occurred to me to check in the bathroom. I knew I had never felt a need to wear my sunglasses in there before, but I thought I'd check just to be sure. I went into the bathroom and looked all around the bathtub and toilet. Just as I suspected—no sunglasses. I turned to glance around the sink and then…um…I, uh, caught a glimpse of myself in the mirror. There the sunglasses were—pushed back on my head. I had been wearing them the whole time. The thing I had been looking so diligently for, I already had. I thought the prudent thing would be to simply tell Melanie I had found them in the bathroom if she asked. She really didn't need more information than that. Thankfully, she didn't ask.

My search for my sunglasses isn't unlike the search many people conduct in an attempt to become more righteous. Many are zealously looking for something they already have. Isaiah teaches us to look to the rock from which we were cut and to the place from which we were taken. In other words, look to your Creator. He is the source of your righteousness.

If you want to find righteousness, it's important to look in the right place. The place to look is to the Rock of Ages, the One in whom we find our very life. The blueprint for your original design can be seen in the person of Jesus Christ. He is the pattern for God's creation of you. If you want to see yourself the way God has designed you to be, look at Jesus!

The hunger for righteousness is a God-given desire that has been met in Jesus Christ. In Him the search is over. For anybody to keep looking for righteousness through what they do is completely unnecessary. It's a waste of time and a damaging distraction.

The Bible is clear about the reality of our righteousness in Christ. First Corinthians 1:30 says, "By His doing you are in Christ Jesus, who became to us wisdom from God, and righteousness and sanctification, and redemption." There is nothing you can do to be righteous because Jesus Christ has already done it for you.

How can you know you are righteous? The verse says it is because Christ Jesus *became* your righteousness. You live in union with Him and, because of that, His righteousness is yours. Just believe it!

Just as we all received sin from Adam, we have received righteousness in Jesus Christ. Romans 5:19 affirms this: "As through the one man's disobedience, the many were made sinners, even so through the obedience of the One the many will be made righteous." Is it by your obedience that you become righteous? No, this verse says that it is by the obedience of Christ that you have become righteous. It is yours because of His life within you.

When the Old Testament high priest offered the sacrifice for the sins of the people to God, the only thing that mattered was the purity of the sacrifice. It wasn't the condition of the people that was examined, but the condition of the sacrifice. That principle is even truer today. Jesus was the Perfect Sacrifice. It is because of what He has done, not what we do, that we have been made righteous. It's a finished work, a done deal. You can relax and simply trust Him!

Some try to find righteousness through their church involvement. Others hope to gain it in their daily Bible reading. Many try to find it in their prayer life. Have you done these things? Self-effort can produce only one version of righteousness—*self-righteousness.*

It's crucial to know that the righteousness you are trying to find is already yours. You can stop looking to become righteous by your actions. You need only to look to "the Head," to Jesus Himself. What you are looking for, you already have because Christ, the Head of the church, is your very life. The search is over, and the only thing left to do is enjoy what's yours through Him.

16

Making Promises to God

As many as are the promises of God, in Him
they are yes; therefore also through Him is our
Amen to the glory of God through us.

—2 Corinthians 1:20

I spent many years with my life revolving around promises. Half the time I was making promises to God, and the other half I was trying to "stand on the promises of God" by appropriating His promises to my circumstances and trying my best to believe that He would indeed keep them.

Do you find yourself doing that too? It's not an uncommon thing, but as I look at the many years I spent either claiming God's promises or making my own to Him, I wish I'd known something. I thought that making promises to Him and standing on the promises He had made to me were a vital part of my daily walk, but I was wrong.

If I had only understood then what the Bible says about the whole matter of promise-making and promise-believing, I could have saved myself a lot of stress and strain. We're never told in the New Testament to promise anything to God. It's not there. The Bible is, however, full of promises that God has made to us. That's the part of grace that people find so hard to accept—it's one-sided. He gives and we get. We have nothing to offer in return, nor is there anything He needs from us. Our only role is to receive all He has promised—but even that doesn't come from our own effort.

Even understanding that God made promises to us isn't enough, because if we don't understand the whole story we will think we have to try to muster the faith to believe He will keep His promises. The truth of the matter is this: God has *already fulfilled* every promise He has made to us! He has done it in Christ.

Paul said that the promises of God are all "Yes!" in Jesus Christ. That means He is the embodiment of God's promises. God's promises to us have been already fulfilled in Jesus! What's our part now? Paul says it is simply to say, "Amen!" Through the life of Jesus Christ in us, we experience the realization of God's fulfilled promises as we trust His Son every moment. Claiming the promises of God is nothing less or more than simply resting in the finished work of Jesus Christ.

In other words, whatever God has promised us, we already have it in Christ. We are "children of the promise" (Romans 9:8), and as "heirs of the promise" (Hebrews 6:17) we can relax and know we don't have to do anything to gain God's blessings in our lives. Everything He has ever promised to do on our behalf has been accomplished and given to us in His Son.

No wonder the apostle Paul praised God by saying, "Blessed be the God and Father of our Lord Jesus Christ, who has blessed us with every spiritual blessing in the heavenly places in Christ" (Ephesians 1:3). Notice that he didn't say that God *will bless* us with spiritual blessings—rather, in Christ we have *already* been "blessed" with every spiritual blessing. The fulfillment of every divine promise will be realized in your life as you simply trust Jesus to be who He is in and through you.

When God got ready to enter into covenant with Abraham as the beneficiary, Abraham (still Abram at that time) went to work to prepare for the ratification ceremony (Genesis 15). He assumed that he and God were about to enter into covenant together.

Abraham prepared the sacrificial animals by cutting them in two and laying the halves on two sides, leaving a bloody path down the middle. Normally, when two people entered into covenant they would walk arm in arm down that bloody pathway together. In so doing, they were promising that they would each keep their part of the covenant, even if it meant shedding their last drop of blood to do it.

But when the time came for the covenant to be ratified, God caused Abraham to fall into a deep sleep. God alone—in the form of a flaming torch and a smoking firepot—walked down the bloody pathway produced by the sacrifice.

What did that mean? It meant that there was no need for Abraham to make any promises. The covenant was made between the Father (fire), the Spirit (smoke), and the Son (blood). Abraham had no part, no role in keeping up his end of the covenant. He didn't have an end to keep up! Keep promises to God? The only thing he would have ended up doing was breaking them anyway. So our Triune God walked the path and entered covenant together, and in so doing, demonstrated that He would keep the terms of the covenant. The only thing Abraham had to do was trust Him by realizing that he was the beneficiary. When it was all said and done, Abraham did believe it and "it was counted to him as righteousness" (Romans 4:3 ESV).

That's all you have to do too. Just believe that Jesus is the fulfillment of God's promises to you in every situation. You don't have to make anything happen. You don't have an end to hold up in this matter. Legalism insists that we "do our part" by working up enough faith to believe His promises or by making promises to Him about how we'll do better and try harder, but grace tells us that He has done it all. We are seated with Christ in the heavenly places. We aren't standing on the promises—we are seated on the premises with Him! So just rest in what He has done and give a loud and hearty "Amen!" to Jesus. That and that alone is what brings the highest glory to God.

17

Distorted Motivation

The love of Christ controls us.

—2 CORINTHIANS 5:14

One day my 11-year-old granddaughter, Hannah, came running to my wife, Melanie, obviously upset. Here's the conversation:

Hannah: Grandmommy, Jeremy just choked me!

Melanie: He choked you?

Hannah: Yes, look at the red mark on my neck!

Melanie: Go tell Jeremy to come here.

Melanie: Jeremy, did you choke Hannah?

Jeremy: (Nods his head yes with a guilty expression on his face.)

Melanie: Jeremy, you can't choke your sister.

Jeremy: I can't go to jail until I'm thirteen.

Melanie: Jeremy, nobody has said anything about going to jail. You don't choke your sister because you love her! Do you love Hannah?

Jeremy: (Nods his head yes again.)

Melanie: Do you think there's anything you want to tell her?

Jeremy: I'm sorry.

Melanie: That's a good idea.

Jeremy goes into the other room and apologizes.

Yes, those are my daughter's children! Jeremy really is a kind boy, and that behavior was untypical of his normal attitude. I'll admit, though, that his train seriously jumped the track with that incident.

It's noteworthy that the first response that popped into his seven-year-old mind was about the law and jail. The little legalist takes after his dad's side of the family. I'm joking, of course, but the issue here is that it is the bent of the flesh to think in legalistic terms. Would it be wrong to do this or that? Would I be punished for doing it?

It's not just Jeremy who missed the point. We all miss it at times. Our actions aren't about right versus wrong or about punishment. The catalyst for our lives is to be love. When our lifestyle is grounded in our union with Triune Love, we live from that benchmark, not from a set of rules that come with a corresponding set of rewards and punishments. We act lovingly because Love is our DNA. In Him we live (and love) and move and exist.

Love relocates the motivation for our behavior out of the realm of duty and into the realm of desire. We honor Christ in our actions because we *want* to, not because we have to. So many people have been abused by a religion that has taught them that they *must* behave in certain ways. They've never been free to live a godly lifestyle. Instead, they have always been obligated to live a certain way.

Your Father's love for you will remain the same regardless of what you do or don't do. However, as long as we think that our behavior has anything to do with how He feels about us, we will never be able to rest in His love. We will always find ourselves focusing on what we're doing, wondering if it is good enough to stay in His good favor.

The wonderful truth about our Father's grace is that He doesn't love you because of how good you are. He loves you because of how good He is. Your behavior may fluctuate, but God's love for you does not. His love for you will never be any greater or any less than it is at this very moment. Your Father loves you like He loves His own Son. In fact, you stand in a Circle of Love among the Persons of the Trinity, and the great Three-in-One embrace you in the same way that the Father, Son, and Spirit embrace each other in an eternal love that will forever be steadfast and unchangeable.

The apostle Paul said it was the love of Christ that controlled his actions. It is important to note that he didn't say it was his love *for* Christ—instead it was Christ's love for him that regulated how he behaved. The emphasis in the modern church is about how we should love Him, but the emphasis of the New Testament is on His love for us. To reverse the two is to find ourselves in a place where we're filled with constant spiritual fatigue from our efforts to love Him more.

Our lifestyles are to be motivated by His love for us, but how are we to grow in our love for Him? The answer is to grow in the knowledge of His love for us. As you grow in your capacity to receive His love, you will discover that love flowing out in your lifestyle in unprecedented ways.

Too many times when we misbehave, we confess and ask God to help us to love Him more. But as we grow in the knowledge of His love for us, loving Him in a greater way will be the natural outgrowth. "We love, because He first loved us" (1 John 4:19). When we know how much we are truly loved regardless of whether our behavior is right or wrong, our motivation changes so that we become motivated internally, not externally.

So, when your own behavior jumps track at times, don't look upward to an imaginary Judge of the Universe who stands ready to send you to jail. Look into the face of Pure Love, and you'll find yourself wanting to behave well on the basis of His loving attitude and actions toward you.

18

Making a Difference
Behind the Scenes

Many who are first will be last; and the last, first.

—MATTHEW 19:30

Recently, a middle-aged man's words to me expressed how many people feel. "I want to impact other people's lives with God's love, but all I do is just go to work, come home, sit around, and then go to bed, only to repeat the same routine the next day, and so on. I see other people making a difference but I don't think I do."

Have you ever felt like you've been left sitting on the sidelines while God is actively blessing others with ministry opportunities that make a difference in the kingdom? If so, you've fallen into a snare that will hinder your grace walk.

The way our Father works through us varies from person to person. It's easy to look at other people and compare their strengths to our own weaknesses. "I wish I were more outgoing. I wish I knew the Bible better. I wish I had that kind of ministry too. I wish…" This is not a productive way to think or live.

Paul was a great communicator of the gospel but even he spoke about the foolishness of making that kind of comparison. "We are not bold to class or compare ourselves with some of those who commend themselves; but when they measure themselves by themselves and compare themselves with themselves, they are without understanding" (2 Corinthians 10:12).

Looking into the Bible, it's easy to see the public ministries of people like Paul or Peter or others, who seemed to find a wide audience who listened to their teachings. It's easy to think that the value of a person's ministry can be measured by the results that can be seen. That's just not true, though.

Do you remember a man named Andrew? He was Peter's brother, and he introduced Peter to Jesus. In Scripture, Andrew appears to be a quiet, unassuming man, but because he introduced Peter to Jesus, God used him to open the door for the Gentiles to hear the gospel through his brother.

Aquila and Priscilla don't often get top billing in sermons, but it seems that much of Paul's success in his public ministry can be linked to this loving couple, who took him under their wing. Who knows how Paul's ministry might have been diminished had God not sent these two to him?

There are many others in the New Testament whose names don't stand out in lights, but there is little doubt that their names are well-known in heaven. I sometimes wonder if these won't be the real heroes of heaven— people who didn't get the recognition here but who quietly yet zealously shared life and love with others, one day at a time.

Don't think that your life isn't making a big difference. God once told Israel, "In quietness and trust is your strength" (Isaiah 30:15). Yours doesn't have to be a high-profile ministry to have eternal value. One person empowered by Jesus Christ can make a greater impact for eternity than a great organization of people who aren't relying on Him.

You may be tempted to think that your life isn't making much of an impact on anybody, but you aren't in a position to know that. The interaction you have with people in your life on a day-to-day basis may seem incidental to you, but in the Father's scheme of things, a word you say or a deed you do for another may ultimately prove to be monumental to them and to the kingdom. Think about your own life. If you're like most people, some of the most significant things you've experienced are statements or actions from somebody who had no idea of the impact of their words or deeds on you.

Paul wrote to the believers at Corinth,

> Consider your calling, brethren, that there were not many
> wise according to the flesh, not many mighty, not many noble;
> but God has chosen the foolish things of the world to shame

the wise, and God has chosen the weak things of the world to
shame the things which are strong, and the base things of the
world and the despised God has chosen, the things that are
not, so that He may nullify the things that are, so that no man
may boast before God (1 Corinthians 1:26-29).

Don't fall into the trap of thinking that you aren't qualified to make
an eternal impact on the lives of others. As Paul told the Corinthians, it is
from your weakness that the glory of God will be best revealed. So don't
discount in your mind what God is doing in and through your life.

We may all discover in eternity that some people whose public shadow
seems large today aren't accomplishing much of real value in God's kingdom and that others who are quietly serving behind the scenes will be the
heroes of heaven mentioned earlier.

You aren't in a position to judge those sorts of things, so don't. Just be
comfortable with who you are and live your life in the way that fits your
personality, your temperament, and your gifts. When you get to heaven,
you may be pleasantly surprised to find out just how much impact that
really had.

19

Abandoning the Religious Rat Race

Come to Me, all who are weary and heavy-laden, and I will give you rest.

—Matthew 11:28

Recently I was told that a pastor I knew years ago had walked into the woods, pulled out a gun, and killed himself. The man was known in his community as a busy, sincere, and hardworking man, but behind the scenes he had struggled with self-doubts and emotional and mental fatigue.

Sometimes there's a short step between spiritual service and the religious treadmill—and that short step makes all the difference. Real love motivates authentic service, while religious laws power the religious treadmill. Desire leads the first but duty drives the latter. It's the difference between a tiring sense of "ought to" and a thrilling sense of "want to."

Are you on the religious treadmill? Get off. You may find it gratifying in the short run, but over the long haul it'll drain you. Self-driven religious fervor becomes a one-night stand repeated over and over and over again. There may be shallow gratification in one-night stands, but nobody would ever mistake them for genuine intimacy.

God offers you much more than that. He wants you to experience Him within the soothing rhythm of grace. However, to know that kind of intimacy with Him, you must stop any religious hyperventilating you've mistaken for a grace walk, calm down, and do what is born from the expression of Christ within you. God doesn't need you to break the three-minute mile for Him. He just wants you to enjoy Him, knowing that everything else in your life will flow out of that.

The fact remains, however, that the religious rat race slowly drains the life out of our intimacy with God. God didn't invite you to be His maid, but His bride. Of course you will serve Him, but it is to be the natural expression of your love for Him. Otherwise, it becomes a stumbling block in your grace walk.

Well-meaning believers often find themselves in a place that can be compared to the man adrift at sea in a life raft. Because he is dying of thirst, he begins to drink the seawater around him. The salt water causes him to become increasingly thirsty, and his thirst causes him to drink more seawater. This vicious cycle will ultimately bring death.

This will be the fate of anybody who believes that doing more is the remedy for his inner thirst. Sometimes the answer to our deepest need is met when we understand that the best way to advance may be to retreat, remembering that God's ways are not our ways.

Blaise Pascal said, "The sole cause of man's unhappiness is that he does not know how to stay quietly in his room." It isn't frenzy, but faith, that facilitates intimacy.

Don't allow yourself to be pressured by the religious machinery so prevalent in modern Christian culture. It's not that you are to become spiritually passive. Christ within you will see to it that no such thing happens. On the other hand, you are free to step away from any demand that you do more than His Spirit is leading you to do.

Don't let other people manipulate you into doing what they think you need to do. That's not their call. That matter rests between you and the Holy Spirit. To stand on this fact sometimes requires that you be willing to accept the disapproval of others who try to pressure you into doing what they think is right for you.

Jesus didn't come to help us be religious superstars. Far from it. He came to deliver us from empty religion—even orthodox, time-honored religion. He came to bring us into intimacy with God through Himself. In His earthly days and in our day, those most offended by Him have been the religionists who have built their reputation around keeping their golden idols polished to a brighter shine than anybody else in town.

The idols are their own particular rules of the religious road race that must be observed as they speed down the highway they call "Christian living." Their display case is filled with the idols that most easily fit their own personality and temperament. They judge everybody else by whether or not they live up to their own self-imposed standards. People and relationships are incidental. What matters is how you are behaving.

Even Jesus wasn't a good churchman by the standards of the religionists of His day. He didn't live up to what they thought He ought to be. To them, He had no convictions. He appeared to compromise the purity and integrity of their values by doing things like healing people on the Sabbath and eating with the crooks (publicans) and party animals (sinners) of His day. He was a friend of the hookers and homeless. He didn't separate Himself far enough from the riffraff, as every good churchman knew one should do. Consequently, He lost His testimony with the Pharisees… an incidental matter which didn't seem to bother Him at all. Jesus cared more about relationships than reputation. He still does.

A legitimate grace walk flows gently like water along a riverbank, refreshing all who happen to come upon it. It isn't a flash flood of activity that honors God. He doesn't lead us that way. Instead He has chosen to make us "lie down in green pastures; He leads [us] beside quiet waters; [where] He restores [our] soul" (Psalm 23).

Get off the religious treadmill and just put your eyes on Him. He will do "the rest" in you. Do the things God asks, but don't confuse His voice with the demanding voice of dead religion.

20

Absurd Forgiveness

Where sin increased, grace abounded all the more.

—Romans 5:20

When Adam sinned in the Garden of Eden, he wrongly assumed his God would be angry. Instead, God came looking for him to take his regular evening walk.

When Abraham sent his wife, Sarah, into Pharaoh's palace to protect his own skin by allowing her to have sex with another man, God told Pharaoh he was on dangerous ground and he'd better get her out of there right now. The next words to Abraham out of God's mouth were to reassure him of the covenant He had made with him. Not a word about his sin.

When Elijah was depressed and afraid and angry and prayed to die, God sent an angel to feed him so he might regain his strength. No shame or blame.

When Peter denied Jesus, our Lord made sure when He rose from the dead to mention Peter by name and to tell the others to make sure Peter knew He was alive. No reference to what Peter had done.

These were giants in the Bible—giants who made horrific choices. In each instance, the love of God swallowed up their sins and foolishness in one great gulp of grace. By human standards, it's absurd.

What have you done that causes you to think God may be disappointed or disgusted with you? Whatever it is, you need to set it aside, because that's exactly what He has done. As ridiculous as it sounds, God isn't interested in what you've done in the past. Your past has been forgiven.

Adam, Abraham, Elijah, Peter, and many other great Old Covenant saints experienced the grace of God before the cross. He has always been a gracious God. But He hasn't just forgiven your sins. Under the New Covenant, you stand in a much better place. He has annihilated your sins, so that it is as if they had never existed at all.

Hebrews 10:1-2 gives wonderful insight into the effect of realizing that our sins have been taken away from us:

> The Law, since it has only a shadow of the good things to come and not the very form of things, can never, by the same sacrifices which they offer continually year by year, make perfect those who draw near. Otherwise, would they not have ceased to be offered, because the worshipers, having once been cleansed, would no longer have had consciousness of sins?

In this passage, the Bible clearly teaches that the Old Testament sacrifices were offered again and again because they could not "perfect" those for whom they were offered. The sacrifice simply covered their sins for a year, but the next year another sacrifice would have to be offered. Why? Because of the imperfection of the sacrifice.

When Jesus offered Himself as the Perfect Sacrifice, He did something that the blood of bulls and goats could never do. He didn't cover our sins by His blood. He took away our sins. To understand that reality is to be set free from the sin-consciousness that is pervasive in the legalistic world of modern Christendom. Your sins are gone! It's true that where sin flourished, grace flourished even more!

21

Golf and Grace

Are you tired? Worn out? Burned out on religion? Come to me. Get away with me and you'll recover your life. I'll show you how to take a real rest. Walk with me and work with me—watch how I do it. Learn the unforced rhythms of grace. I won't lay anything heavy or ill-fitting on you. Keep company with me and you'll learn to live freely and lightly.

—Matthew 11:28-30 msg

Other men often ask me if I play golf. I'm never quite sure about how to answer that question. Can one really be said to play golf if he consistently shoots 100 and doesn't even count his bad shots? Is it still considered playing golf if you need to take a compass with you so you can find your way out of the woods back into the fairway at nearly every hole? Okay, maybe I exaggerate a little.

Could the apostle Paul have been a golfer? He wrote in Romans 7:15, "I don't understand myself at all. I'm not doing the things I want to do, but keep doing the things I hate." A serious examination of the verse proves his statement had nothing to do with golf, but at first glance one might wonder. I've expressed that same sentiment on the golf course many times.

Strangely enough, when I first began to play golf I hated it. It was embarrassing to play with men who had to wait while I was in the woods searching for my ball, or fishing it out of the water hazard. Before I learned to take a whole lot of balls in my bag, I would feel bad when they had to give me a ball from their bags at practically every hole so that I could finish the game.

I determined I was going to play golf well. So I tried hard. I would square off, address the ball, say a short prayer, and swing. I'd swing with all my might. My plan was to make the green in two strokes, if not one.

However, my ball—obviously possessed by an evil spirit—would react the same way every time. It would slice and immediately find the nearest entrance into the woods. Sometimes my club would barely nick the top of the ball on the tee, causing it to fall off and gently roll 20 or 30 feet in front of me. Meanwhile, my partner would have knocked his ball out of sight. I felt he must be thinking I was a little girl, wearing lace underwear and everything. No *man* could possible play golf that terribly.

My blood pressure would shoot straight up, and I would find myself wondering at times if there really was a God. I felt like a pastor friend who'd said he was so bad at golf that he'd eventually given it up and started preaching against it as a sin. Nonetheless, I would determine to try harder on the next hole. I resolved to hit the ball with greater force—to hit straighter, more accurately. But the next hole would produce the same results.

One day on the back nine, an epiphany came to me. I was standing on a tee box waiting for my playing partner to hit his perfect shot. I began to look around at the surrounding scenery. The landscape around me was beautiful. Have you been on a golf course? They are some of the prettiest places you'll ever see.

As I moved through the back nine, I found myself not thinking about my game so much as enjoying the beauty that surrounded me. I was lulled into distraction from the thought of my score and caught up in the sights. My score was already so high that I knew I would once again be in triple digits, so I decided to forget it and just enjoy the beautiful spring day. So I did.

When I came home that day, for the first time I was relaxed and in a good mood. I hadn't played a perfect game, but I had enjoyed a perfect day. Ever since that time, I don't go to the golf course to play a good game of golf. I go to enjoy the companionship of the friends who endure my game and to enjoy the beauty of it all.

My golf game and my life are a lot alike. When I try hard to live the life I imagine God has designed for me, I always find myself off the fairway where life is intended to be played. I find myself in the woods of sin (defined biblically as "missing the mark"), discouragement, and frustration. However, if I just relax and realize I don't have to have a perfect score in my grace walk, I really enjoy life. Some people view golf as a sport. I view it as a game.

Jesus invites us to walk with Him and learn the unforced rhythms of grace. The abundant life He wants us to enjoy comes as we relax and trust Him that life will happen as it's supposed to happen. We don't have to struggle to achieve a good score. God isn't keeping score on us, nobody else really cares, and we cause ourselves needless worry when we think it's important.

Life isn't a test. Jesus said it is a rest. "I will give you rest," He promised. As you move down the fairway of life, take the lesson I've learned about life on the golf course. Don't try so hard. Just relax and enjoy the game.

22

Shame—A Silly Game

Who told you that you were naked?

—Genesis 3:11

For many people, shame may well be the most destructive force that works against them. It is a weapon our adversary uses to paralyze us with fear and insecurity. Nothing more effectively stops us dead in our tracks and brings all progress in our grace walk to a screeching halt.

Shame sneers at us with its sharp point gouging at the raw nerves of our insecurities, challenging us, "Who do you think you are? Look at yourself! How could God possibly be pleased with somebody like you?" When we don't know the truth, our immediate response is to lower our heads, look away from our Father's loving gaze, and then go into hiding.

When Adam and Eve sinned in the Garden of Eden, things changed for them. The Bible says, "The Lord God called to the man, 'Where are you?' He answered, 'I heard you in the garden, and I was afraid because I was naked; so I hid'" (Genesis 3:9-10 NIV). Fear stemming from shame was the immediate result of Adam's sin, and it has been the lingering problem for humanity ever since then.

Adam hid because he was naked. Imagine that. From the moment Adam and Eve were created, they'd never been anything but naked, and it hadn't mattered to them at all because it didn't matter to God. Now, after eating from the forbidden tree, embarrassment and shame enter the human story. Adam and Eve imagined that God wouldn't accept them the way they were anymore.

God hadn't changed at all. He still came for His walk just as He had done every day. But Adam and Eve had changed completely. Sin had perverted their perception of God's character so that they now imagined Him as One who would be angry and punitive toward them.

Remember this important truth: Adam's sin did not change God; it only changed Adam. The same is true about your own life. There is nothing you have done or could ever do that would change how God feels toward you. He is love, and your sin cannot negate that fact. Until you realize that He isn't upset with you, angry with you, or disappointed in you, that He hasn't distanced Himself from you, peace will elude you. Freedom comes in knowing that God doesn't run away because we've sinned.

God didn't run from Adam because of his sin—instead He came *to* Adam, seeking him out *in* his sin. Fail to understand that and you'll find yourself thinking like Adam, imagining a god who retreats from your sins rather than approaching you in your sins to make things right for you. The religious world may tell you that God will remove Himself from your sin, but Adam's situation shows differently. Your Father rushes to you *in* your sin to rescue you from it. That's the very reason for the incarnation of Jesus Christ!

How did God promise to make things right for Adam and Eve? In Genesis 3:15, He spoke to the serpent: "From now on, you and the woman will be enemies, and your offspring and her offspring will be enemies. He will crush your head, and you will strike his heel" (NLT). The offspring He speaks about who will crush the head of the serpent is Jesus. This is the first reference in Scripture to the coming of Christ to deal with sin. Satan would hurt Jesus at the cross, but Jesus would destroy his power. (A wound to the head is fatal.)

Jesus has come and your sin has been remedied. Satan has lost his power over you. The promise of Genesis 3:15 has come to pass!

Sin caused Adam and Eve to become self-conscious, and they decided they needed to embark on a self-improvement program. Thus came the birth of religion—the attempt to make ourselves more acceptable to God by doing the things we think He would require of us in order for us to be acceptable to Him. The whole thing is ridiculous. God accepts us just like we are. Adam and Eve weren't hiding from God—they were concealing themselves from some imaginary god they had concocted in their newly darkened minds.

They were cringing before somebody who doesn't even exist. Can you see the foolishness of the whole thing? From that day in the garden until Jesus came, humanity was trapped in shame and embarrassment.

Jesus came to free us from the dark legacy of shame and embarrassment left to us by Adam. Thanks to Him, there is no condemnation toward us—none. You may feel shame at times, but it's only an illusion. "Even if our hearts condemn us...God is greater than our hearts, and he knows everything" (1 John 3:20 NLT). This verse reminds us that we sometimes can't trust our emotions, but we can trust God. He knows that we are totally forgiven. The shame game is over—finished. It's a silly game we don't ever have to play again.

Once and for all, we can stop fearing some scary god-of-our-own-making who looks at us with disappointment or irritation. It's an infantile fantasy. There is no divine bogeyman under the cosmic bed who's going to come out and get you.

We're all naked, but that's okay with God. He loves you just like you are. You don't have to change. You don't have to be afraid. You don't have to hide. And you certainly don't have to be ashamed. Your Father loves and adores you just the way you are. So come out, come out, wherever you are. Somebody is waiting to give you a hug. He longs to laugh with you. He wants you to feel His embrace and revel in His acceptance for all eternity. Leave shame alone. You belong in the conscious awareness of your permanent place in our Father's embrace. That embrace will transform your life.

23

Trusting Our Hearts

I will give you a new heart and put a new spirit within you.

—Ezekiel 36:26

As the story goes, a young music student once approached Wolfgang Amadeus Mozart and said, "I would like to write a concerto. Can you help me?"

"You're too young," Mozart told him. "Wait a few years."

"But is it not true that you were composing music when you were just seven or eight?" the student persisted.

"Yes," answered Mozart, "but I didn't have to ask anybody how."

People often recognize what is within their heart at an early age. It takes a jaded adult perspective to strip a child of the simple faith to believe that he can be an astronaut or inventor or even president of the United States. Children have no trouble trusting what their heart tells them. Maybe that is part of the reason why Jesus said we must become like a little child in order to live in God's kingdom.

To recognize what is in your own heart is a major step in fulfilling the plan your Father has for your life. Once a person has the capacity to know what is in their heart and, along with that knowledge, possesses a childlike faith to trust their heart, their realm of possibilities expands exponentially. Your dreams and core desires aren't silly. They never were. They have been divinely placed within you. They aren't coincidental—they have been joined together inside you by Divine Design.

To live from the heart is to reconnect with the core desires that have been divinely deposited within you. In rediscovering your heart, you're likely to learn that your gifts and abilities align perfectly with those desires. After all, a loving God who has a master plan for your life has created you.

Living from the heart is different than living from the head. Our minds rationalize, scrutinize, and analyze to determine whether or not our dreams are possible. The mind considers the external factors related to the situation and decides whether or not to pursue the course based on what it perceives to be the probability of a successful outcome. The heart knows no such boundaries—rather, it challenges us to reach beyond natural limitations as if there were no limits to what we might do.

To successfully integrate your faith into your daily lifestyle, you must learn to trust your heart again, as you did when you were a child. Your mind certainly isn't an enemy of your heart, but in a world where we have been programmed to believe that reason alone reigns, it is important to once again lay hold of the dreams of your heart and realize you can trust what you discover there.

How do you recognize the calling of your heart? The answer is closely related to understanding what moves you, what matters most to you. If you want to rediscover your heart, you can find it by identifying the things you value most in life. Your heart isn't interested in becoming rich, but in becoming real—living out of your authentic self. It is what *matters* most, not what pays most, that captures the heart.

One highly successful man said to me, "I can make money, but what I really want is to make a difference." That man was speaking from his heart. The well-known quip about having climbed the ladder to the top only to discover it was against the wrong wall describes a situation that's all too common. We know instinctively that we were created for a higher calling in the workplace than simply to gain prestige, power, and possessions. Blaise Pascal said more than 300 years ago, "The heart has its reasons which reason knows nothing of."

Many people with a church background grew up being bombarded with the Old Testament teaching that "the heart is deceitful above all things, and desperately wicked" (Jeremiah 17:9 KJV). Because they have locked in on that single verse to the exclusion of others, they have come to doubt their own heart, believing it to be untrustworthy. While it is true that apart from God's transforming grace, man's heart is deceitful and wicked, you don't live there anymore. You have been embraced by the grace of God and have been transformed.

God promised in another place, "I will give you a new heart with new and right desires, and I will put a new spirit in you. I will take out your stony heart of sin and give you a new, obedient heart" (Ezekiel 36:26 NLT). As a child of God, that is where you live. Your heart's desire is to be obedient to God and to glorify Him. Why else would you be reading a book like this? Trust your heart. God has transformed it by His grace.

Your heart belongs to Jesus Christ. You have become a partaker of the divine nature (2 Peter 1:4). His life is your life. Your learning to trust your heart will progress in direct proportion to choosing to believe that truth.

And when you have learned to trust your heart, you will find that you become emboldened to experience the next characteristic of a believer who successfully integrates faith into the marketplace. You will be ready to live with gusto, drawing others to yourself (and Christ) by your enthusiasm.

If Christ is your life (and He is), then you can live boldly and confidently, knowing that the One who has begun a good work in you will finish what He has started (Philippians 1:6). Your role is to trust your heart, knowing that Christ indwells it. Step out in faith, knowing that His role is to see to it that you discover and fulfill the mission to which He has appointed you.

24

Love Changes Everything

*Love... bears all things, believes all things, hopes
all things, endures all things. Love never fails.*

—1 Corinthians 13:4,7-8

Jackie is a young woman who lived in the inner-city projects for many years. She led a hard life as a drug addict, and she sometimes sold her body to men to sustain her habit. Some might have blamed it on her upbringing, which had been anything but normal. From the time she was a child, the men in her life had abused and exploited her. Now, as an adult, she trusted no man. None. She was callous. Her language was unusually foul for a woman, and she despised men.

A Christian man was ministering in her community, and one day he met Jackie, smiled, and said hello. Jackie rudely frowned at Don and immediately turned away. The next day Don returned to her community and again smiled and said hello. Again she turned away. However, he was persistent. Day after day he came to minister to her neighbors, and each day he smiled and spoke kindly to Jackie.

After a while, she actually began to think that maybe—just maybe—this guy was sincerely nice. Then the thought would rush into her mind, *But why would he have any interest in me? What does he want?* However, despite her skepticism and suspicions about his kindness, she began to respond to Don a little more each day, until finally she was having conversations with him.

As weeks turned into months, Jackie began to realize something. Don was interested in her as a woman. Not in an inappropriate way either. He seemed to genuinely care for her in the way that a man loves a woman, with a purity that she had only dreamed about until now. Could it be that what she was feeling might be true? Did he really *love* her, as it seemed?

As the thought of being the recipient of this wonderful man's love took root in her mind, Jackie began to change. First, she found she didn't want to use foul language anymore when she talked with him. She began to anticipate his visits each day and would get dressed up, put on her makeup, and even wear perfume. She *wanted* to be pleasing to him. He had never criticized her looks or behavior. To the contrary, from the beginning Don had accepted her just like she was. That itself motivated her to want to change.

As Don shared his love with Jackie day after day, she bloomed. Little by little, she was transformed from a hardened, drug-addicted prostitute into a real lady. The change didn't happen because Don pointed out all her faults, because he didn't. She wasn't transformed because it was what she thought she *ought* to do. His love motivated her to *want* to become the lady she was created to be. Don didn't lay religious rules on her; he just loved her, and his relationship to her caused the change in her as a natural result.

Have you realized the transforming power that comes through knowing that Jesus Christ loves you exactly where you are at this moment? Your religious upbringing may be a haunting voice that criticizes you, causing you to feel a shameful need to do better before He can love you, but don't confuse that for the voice of Christ. He never criticizes, never tells you that you have to change to be loved and completely accepted by Him. He loves you right where you are, no matter what you're doing or not doing. It's amazing. Even at the times you don't love yourself, He does.

This issue is one of the biggest differences between authentic Christianity and the legalistic counterfeit that often calls itself by the same name. New Testament Christianity is as immersed in grace as a fish living in the ocean. Where there is no loving grace present, there is no authentic expression of Christianity. God is love, and Jesus has come to make that love known to us. He loves you at every moment and in every situation in which you find yourself.

The pseudo-Christianity of the modern world focuses primarily on our need to change ourselves to achieve a better standing with God. This loveless brand of legalism will not help you, because it is not biblical Christianity. It is a poser, a counterfeit, an imposter. It can never empower anybody to change because its core value isn't the love of God revealed in Jesus. At its core is the demand for improved religious performance.

Even if you could change the way you behave, it would have absolutely no effect on how God feels about you. He isn't moved by our behavior but by the miraculous *agape* that flows out of Him completely independent of our actions or attitudes. Rules may tell you that you must change to gain His love, but grace tells you that you are loved *right now* and couldn't be loved any more.

Legalism changes nothing for the better. The love of God truly changes everything. If you hunger to see growth in your personal grace walk, abandon every religious thought. Embrace the biblical truth of Divine Love in order to experience the transformation you long to know.

Do you know how much He loves *you*? It is humanly illogical that He should love us so much, but He does. Stop trying to change yourself. That's an empty religious act. You don't have to do that. Just receive His love, and *He* will change you. Until then, enjoy Him. You'll be amazed at the power to change you'll discover rising up in you as you simply accept His love.

25

We're Not in Kansas Anymore

You have not passed this way before.

—Joshua 3:4

In *The Wizard of Oz*, when Dorothy and Toto were lifted from their home in Kansas by a tornado and carried to the Land of Oz, they found a whole new world there. Until then they had existed in a land of black-and-white, but when Dorothy opened the door on this new dimension of living, suddenly for the first time she saw that she had found a land rich with beautiful colors.

As she entered into her new life in that wonderful place over the rainbow, she soon discovered that many things were different than they had been in her old life. Standing in awe of the beauty that was revealed to her, she rightly concluded, "I don't think we're in Kansas anymore."

This is the experience of every person to whom God graciously reveals the reality of our true identity in Christ and what it means to walk in grace. Many have lived for years in a world of empty routine, marked by drab, colorless religious activity that holds no real beauty. We were sincere as we went about the business of doing our daily chores for God. Deep within, however, there was a gnawing hunger, a desire for something more. Many of us wondered at times if what we were experiencing was all there is to life. Surely there must be more "somewhere."

When Joshua prepared the people of Israel to cross the Jordan River to go into the Promised Land, he cautioned them to carefully follow the ark of the covenant, the visible sign of God's presence with them. He made clear to them that they needed to follow God because "you have not passed this way before." In Canaan there would be so much to learn. Everything there would be new—the culture, the food, the language… many other things.

It's the same way for us when God delivers us from the wilderness of self-imposed religious rule-keeping and brings us into the land of grace. We find ourselves in a new world where old terminology doesn't fit. Old methods of living are obsolete. The crass language of guilt, shame, self-effort, and personal determination is replaced with the mother tongue of life that effortlessly flows from our King. We learn to relax in a world where we don't live in tension over being judged for missteps; instead, we gain the freedom to live boldly, knowing that our faith will be affirmed even when we think we have failed.

We couldn't have imagined what the grace walk would look like. It turns out to be better than anything a person could ever have conceived. In the land of grace, it is necessary that our minds be renewed to our new way of life. It takes time to see by experience that the old ways of living don't fit in this new world. Grace isn't simply a truth we add to our life-styles. God's grace expressed through the indwelling Christ becomes our life. He doesn't simply make the landscape of life more beautiful. He is the very air we breathe.

Entering into an understanding of our new world brings about a transformation in the way we think. We will find that the way we see all of life is changed as our minds are renewed by the grace of God. The old assumptions about life that Dorothy held in Kansas had to be scrapped when she arrived in the land over the rainbow. As you move deeper into the land of grace, you will discover that you too will begin to interpret life through a new paradigm. Your adjustment to living in grace will be rewarding if you are willing to have old beliefs removed and replaced by new ones that are appropriate to the new place in which you now live.

The Bible says, "Do not be conformed to this world, but be transformed by the renewing of your mind" (Romans 12:2). The old world is a world of dead morality, where everything is black-and-white. The only thing that matters there is doing your chores and doing them well. Life revolves around laws of cause and effect. To be transformed means to step out of the forms set by the world of morality and be renewed in our minds to the reality of our God's eternal, unchanging, never-diminishing, outrageous love!

In the new world of grace, the only cause for blessings is the goodness of God. He wants to renew your mind to this new way—a life where He blesses you, not because of how good you are, but because of how good *He* is. Purpose at this moment to stop viewing your life through the lens of the old. Be transformed by the renewing of your mind. You aren't in Kansas anymore. You are in the land of grace—a place where God is eager to show you all the beauty He has prepared for you.

Don't try to apply the principles of life you knew before in this new place. They don't fit. Just trust Him. He has the days ahead already planned for you. It isn't your responsibility to navigate your way through life. Just walk with Him. Follow the grace-bricked road and enjoy the journey.

26

Making Music Together

I wait for the LORD, my soul does wait,
And in His word do I hope.

—PSALM 130:5

Give me any of the great keyboard compositions written by Bach and let me sit down at the piano, and I can play every note of the piece. Hand me the overture to *The Marriage of Figaro* by Mozart and I can play every note on the page. That's right, I won't miss a note. When I play the piece for you, there will be only one problem with my effort. I can't play the notes on the page in the order they are written. In other words, I can only sit down and bang on the piano, hitting every note at practically the same time to ensure that at some point I will have struck every key on the piano keyboard.

Can you envision my doing what I'm describing? Banging on the piano like a small child? But what I said initially will be true. When I'm finished, I will have played every note written by the composer…just not the way he intended. That creates a problem. What I would be doing wouldn't really be making music. I would be making a mockery of the composer's original intention.

Sometimes we have a tendency to live our lives that way. The Holy Spirit reveals to us God's plan for our lives in certain ways and we then set out to make it happen. We think that if we just know the plan God has for us, we can make it play out. However, when we try to do it on our own, instead of making music we create a discordant mess.

Abraham did it when God told him that He was going to give him a son through Sarah. The song didn't have the tempo Abraham expected. It moved too slowly for him, so he decided to take matters into his own hands by going to Hagar. Nine months later a sour note named Ishmael came forth.

God's people have often found themselves off-key when they have tried to live independently of Him. Israel one day determined that they would defeat Jericho on their own instead of following the direction of the Composer/Conductor, and they soon found themselves singing the discordant dirge of defeat.

The early disciples were told to wait in the upper room until they were endued with power from on high. Instead Peter took the baton and led the whole group in a stanza of "Let's Elect a New Apostle." Somebody named Matthias ended up as the new note in the symphony of early church history, but he didn't really fit the piece. In fact, he played that one measure in church life and then pretty much was never heard from again. In God's time, Paul became a sustained note the Lord played, one that harmonized perfectly with His Salvation Sonata.

There's a lesson we need to learn and then learn again: We can't make the music. Only God can. He wrote the melody, and He alone is the One who can conduct it.

How does this practically apply to your life? It means that it's important to wait on the Lord. Don't grow impatient because you believe the things God wants for your circumstances aren't unfolding as fast as you think they should. God is the Composer of your life. He writes the notes, and He leads the playing of the composition. When we try to take matters into our own hands, we're acting like a child banging on the piano. There's no way we can turn our circumstances into music.

Impatience breeds problems in life. The Bible often encourages patience in our grace walk. The psalmist wrote, "Commit your way to the LORD, trust also in Him, and He will do it. He will bring forth your righteousness as the light and your judgment as the noonday. Rest in the LORD and wait patiently for Him" (Psalm 37:5-7). *He* will do it, the psalmist assures us. We don't have to make anything happen. Our only responsibility is to commit it all to Him and then trust that His timing is perfect.

Isaiah wrote, "Those who wait for the LORD will gain new strength" (Isaiah 40:31). The word *gain* connotes the idea of an exchange. As we wait for Him to act, our weakness is yielded into the hands of our loving Father, and His strength rises up in us.

Paul encouraged the church at Rome, "Be joyful in hope, patient in affliction, faithful in prayer" (Romans 12:12 NIV). When you have your afflictions sandwiched between joyful hope and faithful prayer, as this verse illustrates, you can be assured that everything is on schedule according to the divine timetable.

Augustine said that patience is the companion of wisdom. Most of us have unwisely created needless frustrations for ourselves by refusing to wait for God's timing. We later regretted it. The question is, "Did we learn from our mistake?"

If you patiently wait on the Lord, you will discover that His timing and His order will create a melody in your life that you could never compose. Don't make the mistake of thinking you have to make something happen. Just keep your eyes on the Conductor and He will tell you when to hit the notes and which ones to hit. When you follow His direction, you will be amazed at the tune of triumph you will hear coming out of your own life. Anything else is nothing more than the flat notes of a faithless lifestyle.

27

Canned Foods and Closed Hearts

He heals the brokenhearted and binds up their wounds.

—Psalm 147:3

My parents were born during the decade of the Great Depression. It was a time when many families in America struggled to put food on their tables. Luxuries became vague memory for most Americans during those days. Finding enough food for another week was the goal for most families.

I grew up hearing the stories about meals consisting of salt pork and biscuits, served with syrup or gravy made from a bit of flour. I must say I'm thankful I didn't have to eat meals like that when I was a child. We never lacked for food.

I did, however, notice something that many people my age may remember about their parents' kitchen cabinets. The cupboard was always filled with canned foods, and the freezer was packed with meat and vegetables. Green beans, creamed corn, navy beans, canned yams, peas of various assortments, applesauce, even hominy lined our shelves. Open the kitchen cabinet doors in the home of my childhood and you would think we were about to have an army come over for dinner. Sometimes before Melanie and I go to the grocery store now, the cabinets look pretty empty. Not so in my parents' kitchen. There was always food.

The funny thing was, much of the food in those cabinets seemed to stay there a long time. I don't think I ever saw the cupboard emptied of it. And as an adult looking back on the situation, I think I get it.

My parents' generation had known what it was like to be without food. Consequently, somewhere deep inside them a voice must have said, "I will never be caught without enough food to eat again." Thus the massive inventory of canned goods. Come what might in life, there would be food in the cabinets.

I think that's how many of us deal with our lives. We have at times encountered circumstances that created a sense of loss or need within us. Because the situation was painful, somewhere deep inside us we said, "This won't ever happen to me again." So we hoarded what we had and shut the cabinet door. We went into self-protection mode.

Some people have been hurt by a friend and have now closed the door on vulnerability. They'll never trust another person as a true friend. Others have had a marriage go sour. Today, they won't completely open up to their mate because of fear. If they give everything, they risk losing everything again. Some have been emotionally burned at church. Now they have lumped all churches into the same hypocritical pile and won't become an integral part of any fellowship of believers.

The hurts differ, but the response is common. Shut the door of my heart and don't risk being hurt or losing what I have. After all, if it happened once...

What "great depression" have you experienced in life? What commodity did you feel you had taken from you when you needed it most? Was it trust? Love? Friendship? What have you lost?

As a result, have you tried to stuff those things deep inside you that you don't want to ever lose again? Are you fearful to take them out? Have you resolved that you'll never find yourself in that kind of situation again?

The healing grace of God can free you from the debilitation of your past hurts. The problem with erecting an emotional wall to keep others from hurting us is that it also blocks us from experiencing love, affirmation, affection, and other positive emotions that we need to feed our souls. In Isaiah 53:4, the Bible says of Jesus that "surely our griefs He Himself bore, and our sorrows He carried."

When the Scripture says that Jesus "bore" our griefs, it uses an interesting word in the original Hebrew: *nasa',* which means "to lift up; to take away." It reminds me of NASA, the acronym for the National Aeronautics and Space Administration, the agency that has directed America's space program.

The Bible says that Jesus Christ has lifted up and taken away your griefs. It is as if they have been ejected into outer space—far, far away from you. You don't have to be controlled by the griefs of your past. Believe that He has taken them away and find healing from their residual effects in your life.

Jesus Christ will be the Great Physician of your wounded heart. The psalmist wrote, "He heals the brokenhearted and binds up their wounds" (Psalm 147:3). Submit your wounded heart to him and allow Him to heal you. What a waste if you were to spend the rest of your life with unresolved pain that He stands ready to heal!

There's a problem with keeping canned goods in a cupboard too long. The food will eventually spoil. Sometimes the cans will even explode. What initially seemed like a good idea is ultimately proven to be the wrong choice.

Don't make that mistake in your life. Open the doors of your heart and make use of what is there. Trust people. When pain arises within you, cast "all your anxiety on Him, because He cares for you" (1 Peter 5:7).

Open yourself up to be vulnerable. Share from your heart with those you love. The "great depression" is over. Don't judge your future by the past. You have much to share. Don't hide it behind closed doors. There's a hungry world around you, and you have what they need.

28

Your Father Will Care for You

Rejoice in the Lord always; again I will say, rejoice!

—Philippians 4:4

I have vague memories of the Cuban Missile Crisis, which happened in 1962 when I was in grade school. Some say it was the closest the United States has ever been to nuclear war. One of the main things I remember is that our church family brought canned food and bottled water and put it under a stairway inside the church building. The plan was that we would all gather together at church if a missile were to be launched against us.

As the adults worked, my young friends and I explored the church building. We sat under the stairs with the stockpile of food and water, and I remember thinking to myself, *This wouldn't be a bad place to stay for a while.* I wasn't worried about the danger at hand. I knew something very bad could happen, but reasoned that my parents would take care of me no matter what. So while the adults worried and prayed and collected bottles of water and cans of food, I laughed and played without a care in the world.

This seemed to be the way of the early church, even in the face of persecution. The second chapter of Acts portrays a group of people who laughed and loved, who shared meals and money—people who enjoyed life by trusting their Father regardless of threats that may have been nearby. Even in the face of danger, joy was the order of the day. They would have fully affirmed C.S. Lewis's claim that "joy is the serious business of heaven."

A spirit of God-centered calmness is often conspicuously absent in contemporary Christianity. When did we begin to take ourselves so seriously? What urgent matters have we allowed to rob us of our playful spirit? We are going to live forever. How important can things really be that won't even be remembered, let alone matter, a hundred years from now? What are we trying to prove by our stress-filled agendas, and to whom are we trying to prove it? There's no doubt about it—most of us need to relax.

Don't be tempted to think that circumstances aren't conducive to an attitude of rejoicing. New Testament believers didn't have it easy either. Acts 16 describes a very hard situation faced by Paul and Silas on the first missionary trip to Europe. They had just finished preaching, when a riot broke out. The Bible describes it:

> The crowd rose up together against them, and the chief magistrates tore their robes off them and proceeded to order them to be beaten with rods. When they had struck them with many blows, they threw them into prison, commanding the jailer to guard them securely; and he, having received such a command, threw them into the inner prison and fastened their feet in the stocks.

> But about midnight Paul and Silas were praying and singing hymns of praise to God, and the prisoners were listening to them; and suddenly there came a great earthquake, so that the foundations of the prison house were shaken; and immediately all the doors were opened and everyone's chains were unfastened (Acts 16:22-26).

With their lives in jeopardy, Paul and Silas sang praises to God. What a display of confidence that their Father would take care of them! They knew that the worst thing that could happen would be that they might soon be taken home to heaven, and that is no threat to the believer!

What threatening circumstance do you find yourself in today? Whatever it is, your Father knows about it and He will take care of you. When we don't maintain an attitude of internal joy that can't be touched by external circumstances, the rhythms of grace in our life get out of step. The music soon stops.

On another occasion, Paul wrote, "Rejoice in the Lord always. Let me say it again, rejoice!" He had obviously learned the value of living on the foundation of our Father's loving faithfulness—because these words weren't written from a villa on the Mediterranean Sea. They were written from a prison cell where, again, he was being held for preaching the gospel. Paul had learned to dance to the blues as well as to an upbeat, cheerful melody in life.

There is something childlike (not childish) about a man who can be at peace when he is in prison. Normally, a child has an inner sense that no matter what is going on in the world around them, everything is going to be okay. After all, they reason, their parents have everything under control.

To rejoice in the Lord doesn't mean you're oblivious to danger, but it does mean you are trusting in the protection of your Father. Your security rests in Him, not in the outcome of whatever circumstance you may find yourself in. You can be confident in Him, not in the outcome of what is happening at the moment. The light of His presence in any circumstance is all the light you need to keep grace-walking, even when you can't see the way.

29

Faith and Candy Bars

*After desire has conceived,
it gives birth to sin; and sin, when it is
full-grown, gives birth to death.*

—JAMES 1:15 NIV

Albert Camus once wrote, "Because I longed for eternal life, I went to bed with harlots and drank for nights on end." Ironically, the very act of sin is a cry to experience life to the fullest. Every person is born with an insatiable thirst for transcendence, the opportunity to experience something that takes us outside ourselves to a place where we are so enthralled that every fiber of our being feels fully alive. We all long to know what it is to experience being one with something bigger than ourselves. But the best we can do by ourselves is to manufacture a mundane monotony that we instinctively sense is a pale substitute for the Life we hunger for.

In an effort to escape the land of Mundane Monotony, we sometimes listen to the sultry sirens that seduce us into sin. We mistakenly believe there is something out there that can scratch the nagging itch in our souls, only to discover after sinning that we weren't itching there at all. Apart from divine intervention, a person can spend a lifetime trying to satisfy a yearning that refuses to be quenched by self-invented means.

James said that we sin when we are drawn away by our desires (James 1:14). Drawn away from what or whom? Temptation is the lure to have our focus be carried away from Jesus Christ. Sin happens when we allow ourselves to turn from Him and to something else in order to try to find life on our own.

When we sin, we soon discover that sin never accomplishes what we really want. Sin can gratify, but never satisfy. It's like eating a candy bar when you haven't had a meal all day. It gives you an instant rush of gratification. You feel suddenly energized and it seems like you've made the right choice...for a short time.

Then the rush disappears, and as your blood-sugar level suddenly and drastically drops, you find yourself feeling weaker and more depleted than you did before you chose a candy bar over a satisfying and nutritious meal. You're left feeling fatigued and unfulfilled once again. You know you need something more substantial and sustaining. It isn't uncommon at such a time to feel a sense of self-condemnation trying to satisfy your hunger with such an unhealthy snack.

It's the same with spiritual hunger. Camus acknowledged that he had searched for life in harlots and drunkenness. Where do you seek to find Life when you are drawn away from Jesus? What cheap substitutes have you been tempted to allow to take His place? It doesn't have to be something as lurid as harlots and drunkenness. It could be something much more respectable. James described the process like this:

> Each one is tempted when he is carried away and enticed by
> his own lust. Then when lust has conceived, it gives birth to
> sin; and when sin is accomplished, it brings forth death. Do
> not be deceived, my beloved brethren (James 1:14-16).

It begins when we experience a hunger within us. Often there is nothing wrong with the hunger itself, but the temptation comes to try to fill the hunger in an inappropriate way. For example, we may try to satisfy the hunger to experience the deep joy that can only come from Christ by seeking the rush that drugs can bring. The desire to be loved—one that our God is more than willing and able to meet—may tempt us to reach out and meet that desire through an illicit relationship. Many a legitimate need that could readily be met by Jesus Christ can become a temptation when we allow ourselves to be carried away to try to have that need met in another way.

Once we have crossed the line of decision to sin (when lust has conceived), we commit the sin. As with eating the candy bar, there may be an immediate sense of pleasure, but it doesn't last. Sooner or later, we experience the death that always accompanies such a choice. One way or the other, it is always a dead end.

There is a subtle danger—sometimes not so subtle—that a legitimate hunger can seek to be met through things that don't look wrong on the surface. Many people have tried to satisfy their hunger for an intimate relationship with Christ by substituting church work. Have you done that? It's often easy to know the answer to that question based on this: If I were with you right now and asked you to tell me about your relationship to Jesus Christ, what would you say? Think about it. What would you say to me?

If you immediately started to tell me about your church and your involvement in church, or your activity on behalf of the poor and homeless, that should be a red flag. There is a big difference between religious activity and a relationship with Jesus Christ. In the culture of the modern church, it becomes easy to substitute what we do religiously for who we are in Christ and what we enjoy each day with Him. Our grace walk is not defined by religious activity but by our union with Him. Of course, authentic spiritual service is an overflow of an intimate relationship with God—but that's not at all the same as religious business that masks as something eternally real.

Whether it's cheap wine or even church work, anything we look to other than Jesus to satisfy our hunger becomes a sin to us. Christ alone will satisfy your hunger. Only He will offer the transcendent pleasure of being fully alive. Don't be drawn away from Him. He loves you and offers you life to the fullest. Anything else is empty calories.

30

Compassionate Gentleness

*Look at the birds of the air, that they do not sow, nor
reap nor gather into barns, and yet your heavenly Father
feeds them. Are you not worth much more than they?*

—Matthew 6:26

As I was sitting in my chair overlooking our patio one morning, I was watching the birds in our feeders outside. We have five feeders and enjoy watching the cardinals, finches, house wrens, redheaded woodpeckers, robins, sparrows, hummingbirds, and even the occasional bluebird.

I had opened the sliding doors to feel the outside breeze. Suddenly something startled the birds and they all took off at the same time. One small sparrow made the mistake of flying right through the doorway into my house. As soon as he came through the door, he turned left and hit the window next to the door. He backed off again and tried to go through it a second time.

Immediately I stood up from my chair and moved to help him. I raised my arms and tried to steer him back to the door, but he simply backed up and pounded himself into the window again, this time even harder.

I knew that the only way I could help this small bird was to cup him in my hands, take him outside, and release him. He obviously didn't understand that my hands reaching for him were intended to help. I scared him and, escaping my grasp, he hit the window again and again.

"Oh no!" I said aloud. "It's okay. I'm just trying to help." He kept right on frantically flitting around, slamming his body into the glass. Finally

I was able to cup my hands over him and gently pick him up. His small body trembled as I gently held him and walked outside.

When I reached the middle of the patio, I opened my hands, and the sparrow flew as far up and away as he could go. I came back inside to clean up the feathers around the window.

Sometimes we are all like that little bird. Something in life causes us to instantly react, and we take a wrong turn. It doesn't take long until we wish we had made another choice, and now we desperately want out of the situation we've gotten ourselves into. The problem is that we don't know the way out, so we start flailing around, trying to do anything and everything we can to escape our scary circumstances. In the process, we sometimes hurt ourselves.

By pointing to nearby birds, Jesus encouraged His disciples not to panic about temporal things in this life. "Look at the birds of the air, that they do not sow, nor reap nor gather into barns, and yet your heavenly Father feeds them. Are you not worth much more than they?" Jesus had a way of making it simple, didn't He? If our God cares about the birds, how much more does He care about us?

When Moses was leading the children of Israel out of Egypt and toward the Red Sea, it seemed they had every reason to panic. There was no way across the vast water in front of them, and Pharaoh's army was closing in from the rear. The natural reaction of anybody in that situation would be to scurry around and try to do something—*anything* that might help.

After hearing from God on the matter, Moses spoke words to the people that were completely counterintuitive to what a normal person would think and feel in such a situation. He said, "Don't be afraid. Just stand still and watch the LORD rescue you" (Exodus 14:13 NLT).

Standing still when our lives seem in peril doesn't make sense from the human viewpoint, but that is exactly what is needed in our lives at times. Like the small bird that flew into my house, we don't understand where we are or what's going on around us.

In this never-before-seen environment, everything scares us. What we don't remember is that our loving God sees what we've gotten ourselves into, and He is moved with compassion to help us. But the independent aspect of our makeup is not wired to relax and receive help. In a desperate attempt to deliver ourselves, we often make matters worse.

I felt sincere compassion for that little bird. I had no intention of doing anything other than to rescue and free him. That's exactly the heart of our Father toward us. If we could only learn that and truly believe it, we would "bang our heads" a lot less often.

Are you in a menacing and fearful situation? Here's what to do: Relax. Stop frantically trying to free yourself. You can hurt yourself and others doing that. "Be still and see the salvation of the Lord" is your best approach right now. The hands that are reaching out to you aren't going to hurt you. Your God is in control. He feels compassion for you. He will gently pick you up and set you free. Trust Him. Don't be scared. Yield yourself and your situation to Him.

There is absolutely nothing in me that could have imagined hurting the little bird I wanted to rescue. The compassionate gentleness of your God is infinitely greater than what I showed to a small sparrow that morning. Trust Him. Yield yourself into His hands. It's going to be all right. He promises.

31

Dead Things

Martha then said to Jesus,
"Lord, if You had been here, my
brother would not have died."

—John 11:21

I recently read a story about a little boy whose pet cat was killed one day while he was in school. His mother was very concerned about how he would take the news. When he got home, she explained what had happened. The little boy turned away and began to cry. "Don't worry," the mother said reassuringly. "Kitty's in heaven with God now." The little boy whirled on his mother and with desperation and anger in his voice yelled, "What's God gonna do with a dead cat?"

That's how we all feel sometimes, don't we? We know God has the situation in His hands, but from our perspective the outcome seems to be unchangeable, and the whole thing appears to have a finality to it that we find completely unacceptable. Despite the fact that we know it's in His hands, we want to scream, "What's God gonna do with a dead cat?" In other words, "Why did it have to end this way?"

Mary and Martha felt the same desperation when they buried their brother, Lazarus. Martha spoke for all of us during the times when our crisis doesn't seem to end with a miracle, but with a misery that screams despair into our emotions and thoughts. Martha—later echoed by Mary—lamented, "Lord, if You had been here..." Do you feel that way about situations in your life? Does it seem like there have been times when Jesus wasn't in town when you needed Him the most?

At times we have no clue about the "why" behind God's actions—or, more often it seems, His lack of visible action—in our circumstances. In John 11, the Bible shows that Mary and Martha faced this very dilemma.

The text tells us,

> Now a certain man was sick, Lazarus of Bethany, the village of Mary and her sister Martha. It was the Mary who anointed the Lord with ointment, and wiped His feet with her hair, whose brother Lazarus was sick. So the sisters sent word to Him, saying, "Lord, behold, he whom You love is sick." But when Jesus heard this, He said, "This sickness is not to end in death, but for the glory of God, so that the Son of God may be glorified by it." Now Jesus loved Martha and her sister and Lazarus. So when He heard that he was sick, He then stayed two days longer in the place where He was. Then after this He said to the disciples, "Let us go to Judea again" (verses 1-7).

Jesus' reason for waiting two more days before coming to Bethany makes perfect sense to us now, since we know the whole story. God received greater glory through Jesus' raising Lazarus from the dead than He would have if Jesus had healed him. That possibility wasn't one that would have occurred to these two sisters at all, so how *could* it have made sense to them? All they could see was that their friend wasn't coming through for them when they needed Him the most.

We all feel like these two at times, don't we? You may have faced situations in your life where you have struggled to understand why your prayers seemed to be ignored. It seemed to you that, at a time when you most needed His intervention, God was inactive.

In moments like that it is important to remember that your perspective is limited to what you can see at the moment. Mary and Martha couldn't imagine how their situation could possibly have had a good ending, but God had one in mind all along. You can be assured that the same God who raised Lazarus from the dead is fully aware of your problems.

From your finite understanding, you too may not be able to imagine how your situation could possibly end well, but remember this: You don't see things from the eternal perspective. Your Father does, so trust Him. He has not forgotten, nor is He ignoring you.

There actually is an answer to the question, "What's God gonna do with a dead cat?" One possibility is, He may resurrect it. Dead things don't deter God. He can put life right back into something that is already dead. Hope isn't gone just because a situation appears to have come to a final end.

Or, God may not resurrect it, but may instead redeem it. In other words, He will use the disappointments and devastations of our lives to accomplish a greater purpose. We don't know what's good and what's bad for us. Only He does. What we do know is that our Father loves us. He isn't sadistic, but gently and tenderly loves us at all times. Never do we need to believe this more than when life makes no sense.

When circumstances spiral downward and God doesn't step in to change them, He can—and will—use the outcome in a positive way. We don't have to know how He plans to do it for it to be true. Faith means that we trust Him even when our senses tell us all hope is gone.

Our faith is in our God, period. Faith doesn't require believing that we will get what we want. Instead, it knows that we will get what God wants and that what He wants will be the absolute best. And faith is being willing to accept that and rest in it even if our emotions and thoughts argue with it.

So "what's God gonna do with a dead cat?" Whatever He wants. His role is to be in charge. Ours is to trust.

32

Dealing with Our Fears

Do not fear, for I am with you;
Do not anxiously look about you, for I am your God.
I will strengthen you, surely I will help you,
Surely I will uphold you with My righteous right hand.

—Isaiah 41:10

General Norman Schwarzkopf is a man few people would call any-thing but courageous. One time in an interview he was asked, "General Schwarzkopf, is a general allowed to feel fear?" His answer was, "Sure, I hope so."

Schwarzkopf sometimes talked about how it's not the feelings of fear that are wrong, but it is wrong when we embrace those fears so we find ourselves unable to perform whatever the duty at hand may be. He challenged those he led to understand that courage doesn't mean that one feels no fear, but that true courage is feeling afraid and doing the job anyway.

It is quite common in mainstream Christianity to hear the suggestion that it is wrong to even feel afraid. Now, few things can steal your peace in life faster than being told that you're wrong to have normal human emotions. The faulty notion that it's wrong to feel the emotion of fear has caused people to feel condemned for experiencing those feelings. When Jesus told His disciples not to be afraid, He meant they weren't to embrace those emotions and allow fear to control them. He didn't mean they were wrong for experiencing the spontaneous feelings that circumstances would evoke at times.

It is unrealistic to think you won't experience feelings of fear. While it is true that God has not given us a spirit of fear (2 Timothy 1:7), don't think this means that fear won't sometimes show up on your doorstep asking to be let in. The question is, what are you going to do when it arrives?

You may be tempted to think, *I shouldn't feel this way*. No, feeling afraid is normal in certain circumstances. The apostle Paul once wrote, "I was with you in weakness and in fear and in much trembling" (1 Corinthians 2:3). When Paul faced the daunting assignment to go to Corinth and establish a church, he felt fear, but he acted anyway. Courage isn't the absence of fear, but acting boldly in the face of fear.

When Jesus was in the Garden of Gethsemane on the night before His crucifixion, He experienced feelings of fear. It would be foolish to think otherwise—He was a normal human! What else would cause Him to sweat blood and ask His Father if there was any way for Him to take away what was to come? The pivotal moment in that garden was the way He faced His fears.

Jesus faced His fears, and then acted in faith. He didn't succumb to them. Instead, He courageously moved through them toward the divine purpose of His life. He refused to give in to feelings of fear and, instead, moved forward with faith in His Father.

In Isaiah 41:10, God gives three reasons why we don't have to be afraid when we face threatening circumstances. First, we aren't to fear, because He is present with us. "I am with you," He says. That reality alone is enough to infuse power into our lives when we feel fear. As the apostle Paul once asked, "If God is for us, who can be against us?" (Romans 8:31 NIV). Nothing can separate you from His love—He is present with you in every situation you will ever face.

Second, there is no reason for us to be fearful because God is preeminent over us. "I am your God," He affirms. He isn't indifferent or incapable of dealing with the affairs of our lives that overwhelm us. He stands supreme over our lives and the things that seem to threaten us. Not only is He with us, but our Father also has authority over everything that happens to us.

Finally, He is proactive for us. He assures us that "I will strengthen you, surely I will help you, surely I will uphold you with My righteous right hand." What certainty! Not only is He with us and supreme over the things that happen to us, but He also assures us He will proactively act in our lives when things seem overwhelming. Your God will not stand by indifferently and leave you to navigate your way through the painful times of trouble. His Spirit within you will strengthen and help you. You will not fall to the status of helpless victim to your problem, because He will uphold you and see to it that you pass through the situation and come out victorious on the other side. Remember, He is your Victory in every situation of life.

Your greatest threat is not fear. Your greatest threat is inactivity because of fear. You will feel fear at times. But will you face your fears and move through them, trusting God as you go forward with knocking knees or a fluttering stomach?

If you feel fearful about certain situations, well, welcome to the human race! Don't judge yourself for having feelings that are universal to human beings, but remember that you don't have to embrace them either. You have the life of Jesus Christ in you. By His power, face your fears and then move ahead with the confidence that your Father will guide you each step of the way through the threatening situation you face.

33

Dealing with Sins in Our Lives

The strength of sin is the law.

—1 CORINTHIANS 15:56 KJV

Have you ever been on a diet? I've dieted many times in my life and found one thing to be true. I've asked others about this thing and many have said they've experienced it also. When I'm dieting I find myself craving the foods that I know aren't good for me. That I tell myself I can't have them only causes me to want them more.

Of course, I know that a strict diet isn't the recommended way to lose weight and keep it off, but like the majority of people who want to thin down, I've attempted it anyway. The many diets I've tried haven't taught me much about health and nutrition, but they sure have taught me a lot about the power of the law in our lives.

Here I speak of "the law" in the sense of religious rules. Despite what we may have believed, religious rules don't help us live a godly lifestyle. To the contrary, Paul wrote that sinful actions are actually strengthened by the law. The dietary parallel to this spiritual reality is to tell a man he cannot, under any circumstances, eat pizza. Then guess what food he is constantly drawn to eat. That's what law does…in any context.

The world of religion prescribes religious rule-keeping as the way to deal with sins in our lives. A casual glance at the sermon and Bible-study book selection in the typical Christian bookstore or on the typical Christian website will quickly show one thing: Any reasonable person would come to the conclusion that the most important subject in the church world is to understand how to overcome sin. It seems that most of the information directed toward us about our spiritual walk deals with how to stop sinning and behave better. "Sin management" often seems to be the reason for public ministry, and it seems to be the primary goal many who follow Jesus have embraced for their lives.

Overcoming sinful actions consumes the thoughts and energies of many sincere believers. They are completely dedicated to stopping the wrong things they do and replacing those actions with actions that glorify God. While their motives are certainly sincere, their goal and focus are completely misguided.

Paul wrote about this matter in Romans 8:6: "The mind set on the flesh is death, but the mind set on the Spirit is life and peace." To focus on the wrong things we do is to put our attention on fleshly things. Paul said that to do that moves us in the opposite direction of experiencing God's life and peace within ourselves. It's a matter of badly misplaced focus.

The message of New Covenant grace doesn't exhort us to focus our attention on our sins and our concerted effort to extinguish them. In fact, to take this approach not only won't reduce sinful actions; it will actually increase wrong behavior in our lives. The truth of the matter is, the Bible teaches we aren't to focus on sins at all, but to focus our attention undividedly on Jesus Christ.

Paul dealt with our focus when he warned the Colossian church, which he had established in grace, to not make sins their focus, but instead to look to Christ: "Set your mind on things that are above, not on things that are on earth" (Colossians 3:2 ESV).

Is there some sin from which you want to be free? To try to overcome that sin by focusing on it will have the exact opposite effect you want. If you fixate on what you do wrong and struggle to conquer the bad behavior, you always arrive at some sort of plan that involves your own willpower and determination.

When that happens, it doesn't matter how sincere you might be—you are setting yourself up to fail. Taking an approach that contradicts what the Bible says about your sins won't work, despite the fact that you are sincere and even ask for God's help. He will not help you with your fleshly method. Instead He will let you fail until you come to the place where you are willing to learn and accept His answer for your sinful actions.

Any approach we take to overcome our own sins through self-discipline is legalistic because it stirs up within us the false hope that there is something *we* can do to defeat them. The reality is, *we* don't have to conquer our sins—because Jesus Christ already has defeated sin. When we try to do what He has already accomplished, we are denying the sufficiency of His grace and are substituting a self-glorifying legalistic method. Legalistic methods always doom us to failure. Paul wrote in so many words that sinful passions are aroused by the law (Romans 7:5). He warned the Corinthians, who were trapped in sinful behavior, that "the strength of sin is the law" (1 Corinthians 15:56 KJV).

Legalistic attempts to overcome sins by self-imposed rules and self-determination are to sins what gasoline is to a flame. They won't stop sin, but they *will* make matters worse. The only way to enjoy victory over sin is to rest in the victory that is already yours because of Christ's finished work. He succeeded in permanently defeating sin once for all for our sakes. Transformation will come to your lifestyle as you simply believe that reality and stop trying to do something that Christ has already done. Simply rest in His victory and direct your attention to Him. As you do that, the sins that have wielded power over your lifestyle will fall aside, powerless.

34

Disguising Doubts as Belief

The Lord said to Moses, "Why are you crying out to Me?
Tell the sons of Israel to go forward."

—Exodus 14:15

I haven't seen God answer my prayer yet, but I'm still believing Him for the answer." I often hear this statement made by sincere people. I understand the expression and have even used it myself at times. There are times we do patiently wait for the Lord to act in our lives so that we realize the fulfillment of our prayer requests. On the other hand, sometimes we conceal doubt under the guise of belief.

Consider the situation of Moses in Exodus 14. He had just led the people of Israel out of Egypt and down toward the Red Sea. They looked back and saw that Pharaoh had changed his mind about letting them go. Now his whole army was in hot pursuit of these Jews who followed Moses.

It was a tough place to be. Behind them was an advancing army. In front of them was the Red Sea. The response of the people was to complain and blame Moses for their plight. "We would be better off still serving as slaves in Egypt than to come out here and die!" they argued. "What are we going to do? What are we going to do? What are we going to do?"

Exodus 14:11-14 tells the story:

> They said to Moses, "Is it because there were no graves in Egypt that you have taken us away to die in the wilderness? Why have you dealt with us in this way, bringing us out of Egypt? Is this

not the word that we spoke to you in Egypt, saying, 'Leave us alone that we may serve the Egyptians?' For it would have been better for us to serve the Egyptians than to die in the wilderness."

But Moses said to the people, "Do not fear! Stand by and see the salvation of the LORD which He will accomplish for you today; for the Egyptians whom you have seen today, you will never see them again forever. The LORD will fight for you while you keep silent."

I can imagine Moses responding to them in his most "pastorly" voice. "Don't be scared! Just wait and watch what God does! He is going to deal with this situation. Everything is under control!"

Then Moses must have gone behind a rock and, like them, cried to God, "What are we going to do? What are we going to do? What are we going to do?" We know this must be what happened because of what God said to Moses in the fifteenth verse: "Why are you crying out to Me? Tell Israel to go on forward! And you—lift up your staff and stretch out your hand over the sea and divide it."

God's answer to Moses is clear. "Why are you crying for Me to give you something in this situation? What you need is already in your possession. YOU do something!"

How many times do we face situations where we pray for God to help us and then profess that we are believing and waiting for God to act, when the reality is that we already have in our possession all that we need? Our unwillingness to move forward in faith is really evidence of our doubts, which we hide under a profession of faith.

Fears in our lives can be very subtly hidden at times. It is even possible to spiritualize our response to a situation so it masks our fear in a way that makes our response look almost noble. Don't fall for that trick. It's important not to deceive ourselves into thinking that what we are doing is motivated by faith when the real issue is one of fear. If we aren't sure, which may be the case at times in our lives, we can pray about a matter, and the Holy Spirit will show us the answer as time goes by. He will begin to give clarity to our focus so it will become evident to us whether fear or faith is the underpinning of our spiritual posture. Once we know the answer, it's important to act on that knowledge.

Are you waiting for God to do something in a particular situation? Maybe He is waiting for *you* to do something! You have everything you need for this life through Jesus Christ. Paul reminded those at Colossae, "In Him you have been made complete." The word *complete* suggests being liberally supplied so that nothing at all is lacking.

In Jesus Christ, you have everything necessary to complete what He puts before you to do. While there certainly is a balance between impulsive action and paralysis because of fear, don't say you believe if you aren't willing to act when it's time to act. You may be holding in your possession right now all you need to solve your problem and see your prayer immediately answered. Don't hide your doubts under a profession of faith. Act in boldness and watch what your Father will do through you. It may be time to stop praying and professing...and simply proceed. Go forward!

35

True Value

You have been bought with a price.

—1 Corinthians 6:20

Imagine you've arrived to attend a meeting. As you walk through the parking lot at your meeting place, you see something on the ground that sparkles. It turns out to be a ring, and it has what appears to be a big diamond in a setting that looks like white gold.

What would you do? Most likely you would bring it inside to the meeting and try to find out who owned it. Imagine that, in this case, nobody claims it and the group agrees, "You found the ring. No one has claimed it, so it's yours to keep." As you look at it, you estimate the gem to be about a one-carat diamond. Immediately you think what most people would: *I wonder what it's worth.*

You ask your friend seated beside you what she thinks the diamond is worth. She exclaims over its beauty and tells you it's worth about 6000 or 7000 dollars. Then you take it to another friend and she says, "No, that's no diamond. That's cubic zirconia. I think it is only worth about 300 dollars." You take it to yet another friend, who looks at it and says, "No, I don't think that's even a real stone. That's just plastic. Why, that's not worth more than about 4 or 5 dollars."

At this point you have valuations of the ring that range from $4 to $7000. How can you know its value for certain? You can take it to a qualified appraiser. He or she will set a value on it based on the price someone would be willing to pay for it. If somebody were willing to pay $5000 for the ring, then its value is $5000. You could look at the ring and say, "This ring equals $5000." The ring and the $5000 have the same value.

When we came into the world, we were all born with a big question mark over our heads. The question was, *What is my value? What am I worth?* Unless you know your identity in Christ, you are always asking in one way or another, *What is my value? What am I worth?*

We don't verbally ask people that question, but the way we relate to them is an attempt to establish in our own minds what our value is, and we base it on what other people tell us about ourselves. (We probably get varying appraisals, depending on whether we ask our mother or our employer.)

Sadly, that's how most people go through life…trying to assure themselves that they really are worth something to somebody. It's a sad and misguided way to live. The fact is, there is a way you can know your value. Bring yourself before the expert. Come to God and say, "Can You tell me my value?"

God will answer, "Yes, I can." He will then determine your value the same way the appraiser determines the value of the ring. It hinges on what price someone is willing to pay for you. In this case it's not hard to figure out.

God says, "You have been bought with a price. And I am the One who bought you. What I paid for you is the life of Jesus." Isn't that response a biblical one? Then would it be accurate to say that to God, you are of equal value to Jesus? It almost sounds blasphemous, doesn't it? It isn't, though. You can be assured that your heavenly Father treasures you like He treasures His own Son, because Christ is your life. You are one with Him.

Therefore, you have tremendous value. I'm not talking about your behavior. Maybe your background has caused you to think that your value in life is connected with what you do. People are often validated in the business world based on their accomplishments. Those who work hard and achieve much are often lauded as significant people.

The same approach is found in the church world. Many people wrongly believe that their value to God depends on their religious activity. Nothing could be further from the truth. Your local congregation may seem to value those who work hardest and longest, but that approach is simply a religious one, not a biblical one.

God doesn't value you based on what you do or don't do. In fact, the Bible declares in Romans 5:8, "While we were yet sinners, Christ died for us." When humanity was at its worst, God showed us how much value He placed upon us by giving Himself to deal with our sin and bring us into a loving relationship with Himself.

So to speak about your worth isn't to focus on what you do or don't do, or can or can't do, in any area of your life. To discuss your value—your authentic value—is to examine your core nature. It's a reference to who you are, and to your worth in the eyes of your Creator.

The cost for you to become a part of the circle of love existing between the Father, Son, and Holy Spirit was the very life of Jesus, but it was a cost well worth it to our Triune God. That's how much He loves you. His love defines your value. Don't fall into the trap of seeing yourself through the murky, distorted lens of performance. Other people may judge you based on external factors, but the One whose opinion defines you has judged you to be of inestimable value because of the Internal Life, Christ Himself, from whom you gain your very identity.

36

Don't Give Up!

...fixing our eyes on Jesus, the author and perfecter
of faith, who for the joy set before Him endured
the cross, despising the shame, and has sat down
at the right hand of the throne of God.

—Hebrews 12:2

What's the point?" the young man asked me. He sat slumped in his chair, staring at the floor without blinking. He had lapsed again into his struggle with addiction and was obviously not optimistic about ever being free. He was the classic example of someone who was on the edge of giving up completely.

Sometimes it really does seem that the easiest thing to do is to just give up. When we face the temptation to quit, lies flood our souls. Lies point out every deficiency in us that we are willing to entertain, both real and imagined. At that moment, our weaknesses seem to be what defines us. We look backward at all the times we've renewed our efforts, only to fail again. Because we can't imagine things any different, we see our future in bleak, dreary terms—self-definitions that try to strip away any hope that our present course could possibly lead to a good outcome.

Our emotions are under assault. The inclination is to let ourselves be weakened and depleted physically, mentally, emotionally, and spiritually. Through wearing us down, our spiritual enemy hopes to go for the knock-out at the right moment.

If you've ever felt that way, it's important to know that you aren't alone. We've all felt that way at times. Jesus, who was tempted in every way that we are, also faced the temptation to give up.

Shortly before He was crucified He found Himself in the Garden of Gethsemane, battling the forces of darkness. Being fully human, He felt fully human emotions. He must have felt dread over the events He knew were to come in a few hours.

He had seen the spiteful anger of the religious leaders and had watched the cowardly political correctness of the government leaders—all those who had control over His ultimate fate, from a human standpoint. What was soon to come was obvious.

In the garden, Jesus prayed the prayer any man in His situation would pray. He prayed for the threat that lay ahead to disappear. The thought of being crucified was appalling to His natural, human emotions.

However, in His weakness, Jesus never lost focus on His Father or on the purpose for which He had come. After grappling with the full spectrum of negative human emotions, He did what He now empowers you to do. He didn't quit. He yielded Himself to the Father's purpose for Him and squarely faced the events of the unfair trial and the horrific crucifixion. The Bible says that He "endured the cross, despising the shame." Don't think for a moment that after He decided to face the cross, things became any easier. He *endured* it.

Enduring trouble in life is Christlike. Don't think when you are facing great trials that if you had the right kind of faith you would feel better about what you're facing. At no moment, I believe, did His emotions feel to Him like He was doing the right thing. It was the knowledge of the joy that was to come that caused Him to persevere and reject the taunts and temptations to "come down from the cross." It was because He knew that once His work on the cross was complete, He would have faithfully fulfilled His divine mission.

Authentic faith doesn't make your trials any less painful. The circumstances will hurt—but don't quit. Don't give in to the lies. Persevere. The Bible says that the Lord orders the steps of a good person. He will lead you through the difficult terrain you may be struggling through now. He will not abandon you or leave you to find your own way.

When you are tempted to give up, it becomes easy to think of reasons why you aren't suited to move ahead through trying circumstances. You see the challenges before you as monumental and your own weaknesses as disqualifying. In that moment of temptation, remember that your challenges aren't to be compared to your own abilities, but to the ability of the omnipotent God you serve.

Despite any limitations you may have, you are not a quitter. Your faith in Christ is all you need, and it doesn't even have to be "great faith." Even a cry of desperation directed toward Him is a prayer of faith. When choosing to persevere feels like you are trying to wade against the current of a fast-moving river, choose to act like who you are. Call upon the Christ who indwells you and press onward. He has already conquered the greatest enemy, and He will empower you to be victorious in the battle with the enemy who rages against you.

A grace walk is a divinely empowered walk. It is one in which you have the capacity to rise above feelings and thoughts that would cause you to move in the wrong direction—and choose the path that God has called you to walk. You have divine enablement within you. Depend on Him.

Don't be tempted to reach down into your own humanity, your own ability, and your own self-confidence to keep on going. None of those resources are sufficient to sustain your forward momentum. Choose by faith to depend upon the One who lives inside you. Acknowledge your weakness and appropriate His strength. Those who do will find that instead of crashing, they "get fresh strength. They spread their wings and soar like eagles. They run and don't get tired, they walk and don't lag behind" (Isaiah 40:31 MSG).

You may think you don't have enough faith to persevere, but He alone is the "perfecter of [your] faith." Again, *you don't have to have great faith.* You only need to depend on the One who lives inside you. His faith is enough for the both of you. His faith is your faith. When you feel like your faith is weak, remember, "the life which I now live in the flesh I live by the faith of the Son of God, who loved me, and gave himself for me" (Galatians 2:20 KJV).

Perseverance that is Christ-empowered will see you through. Whatever your circumstance may be, don't surrender to it. Lean into Him as your Source. You aren't made—God didn't make you—to give up under pressure. Look beyond the immediate stressful factors and see a better day ahead. It will most certainly come. Until it does, choose to persevere and, by God's grace, follow through with your decision.

37

Eyes That See

He turned to his disciples and said privately,
"Blessed are the eyes that see what you see."

—Luke 10:23 NIV

I was visiting with Dan, a pastor friend from Iowa, when he began to explain to me how he trained horses using the methods developed by Buck Brannaman, "the horse whisperer" (the actual man about whom the Robert Redford movie was made). Shortly into our conversation, he took out a videotape with footage of a horse being gentled using that method.

As we watched, Dan pointed out how the way the trainer worked with the wild horse closely paralleled the way the Holy Spirit works in our lives, bringing us into submission to God and teaching us His love for us. "Watch him," Dan said about the horse. "The trainer has run him in a circular corral until he's figured out there's no way out. You'll see him start bowing his head toward the ground as a sign of submission to the trainer." As I watched the video, that was exactly what happened. "Now look," Dan continued. "His ear will turn in toward the trainer. Although he hasn't yet learned to completely trust the trainer, he wants to hear him."

I sat there dumbfounded by what I saw. There were lessons in plain view that this horse was teaching me about my relationship to God. As Dan explained what was going on between the trainer and the horse, there was no doubt about it—I saw God clearly in that picture, that metaphor. When the video ended, I felt like I had "been to church."

The idea that God can speak to us only through the Bible is one of the biggest deceptions people buy into. There are many "ministry metaphors" in your everyday routine that can be used by the Holy Spirit to encourage you with an awareness of your Father's loving grace. Certainly He will never speak in a way that contradicts Scripture, but the variety of ways He can communicate with you are limitless.

If you have believed that the only way you can hear the voice of your Father is via "religious" means, ask Him to reveal Himself to you in your daily routine. Learning to see Him in the details of daily living will bring you a deeper sense of intimacy with Him than you could ever know otherwise.

When Jesus taught, He often pointed to fishnets, fields, trees, birds, and other things and people around Him. He pointed to the environment in which His hearers lived to show them His Father. He still does the same today for those who have eyes to see and ears to hear. Open your eyes and be aware. It isn't necessary to try to find hidden spiritual meaning in everything around you. Your openness to seeing your Father's loving face in the details of the world around is all that is necessary. He will do the rest.

38

The Offense of Grace

It was right to be glad and to have a feast;
for this your brother, who was dead,
is living again; he had gone away
and has come back.

LUKE 15:32, BIBLE IN BASIC ENGLISH

The one thing about grace that many people have a problem with is this: It appears to be carelessly and indiscriminately thrown around by our heavenly Father, as if there is no limit to it and He doesn't care who receives it. By human standards this just isn't right. After all, fair is fair. Give people an inch and they'll take a mile. Go soft on those who have sinned, and the next thing you know everybody is doing it. People make their beds and they should lie in them. They need to learn their lesson. After all, you've got to think about the message you're sending!

All religions are built around the idea that good deeds are rewarded and bad deeds are punished. Many people have even distorted authentic Christianity into a religion of checks and balances revolving around reward and punishment. After all, isn't that how life works?

To answer that question, it *is* how life works that has been built around a judicial system of this world, but it's not how things work in the kingdom of God. As popular as the reward-and-punishment view might be, that isn't how authentic Christianity looks. Law rules this temporal world, but grace is the template by which God rules.

Grace is the thrilling (or, to legalistic religionists, horrifying) news that

God isn't into payback for the wrong things we've done. That isn't to say that we may not still reap the consequences of wrong things we do, but the grace gospel clearly announces the good news that our Father isn't in the business of balancing some kind of morality ledger by punishing us when we've done something wrong. He's not a divine bookkeeper trying to make sure that the "punishment-doled-out" account is equal to the "record of misbehavior" account.

The story of the way the father treated his prodigal son should put that misunderstanding to rest. In Jesus' famous parable we find a hyper-religious zealot's worst nightmare. Imagine it this way: A young man in the youth group decides he wants to leave it all and move away. He asks his father to give him his inheritance (an insinuation that he's been thinking he'd be better off if his dad were dead), and off he goes to the big city. His life soon becomes a blur of all things he had been warned against as a child.

Eventually all his money is gone and the young Jewish man wakes up as a food-flinger in a pigpen. (Maybe we can compare this to a boy from a good Christian family ending up as a dishwasher in a strip joint.) He's jolted back to reality. *I'm out of here*, he thinks to himself. *Even Dad's minimum-wage guys at home don't have to live like this.*

You know how the story ends. The moment comes when this scraggly looking, nasty-smelling son comes stumbling up the long driveway. His dad catches sight of him and immediately tears out running at full throttle.

The neighbors must have been horrified. First, it would have been a very undignified thing for a grown man to run like that. Propriety would have demanded that the father wait for the son to come to him. But that's not what the father did. He ran to his son—and abandoning all dignity, he ran fast.

To run also required a clothing adjustment. Like all fathers in that part of the world, this man wore long, flowing robes. In order to run, he had to pull the robes up between his legs, above his knees. As if running weren't shameful enough, now the man was exposing his naked legs for all to see. This was the height of shamefulness! A running old father! Partial nudity! What was the respectable neighborhood coming to now?

This father didn't care. He was, in essence, drawing the shame of his approaching son off the boy and taking it onto himself. The only thing that would shock the neighbors more than the son's behavior was the behavior of the father! The foolishness of the son dissipated in the presence of the father's loving actions. Maybe that was the father's point. Grace always is bigger than sin, and people have always needed to learn that.

The father then grabs hold of his boy and, oblivious to the stench of the pigpen, starts laughing and crying, hugging and kissing him, all at the same time. The son is forgiven before he even asks.

The boy chokes up and tries to talk. This isn't what he had expected. He gets out half a sentence before Dad interrupts and yells orders to fire up the grill, call the family and friends, see if JJT is available (the Jerusalem Jazz Trio), and let's get this party started!

Some—perhaps many—must have thought, *That's a strange story, Jesus. Don't You think it might give the wrong message?*

"No," our loving Savior would answer. "It gives the right message. The message is this: It doesn't matter how pathetic you are, how low you have gone, and how long you have been there—I love you and accept you."

The religionists of Jesus' day were just as concerned about the implications of a story like this as they are in our day. They feared it might sound like this sort of grace would give people a license to sin. They were indignant that the story communicated that somebody got away with something. They assumed this kind of grace would actually encourage, rather than discourage, sinning.

Jesus didn't seem to worry about all that when He told this story… or in His ministry in general. He just loved people and poured out grace, grace, and more grace on the most unlikely candidates. It galls the self-righteous when their sense of justice is violated, but Jesus never seemed to care about what they thought. He seemed to show such little discernment in how and to whom He gave so much. Even His stories seemed to communicate a message that sounds downright wrong to religious ears.

Is it possible that grace is counterintuitive to the religious mindset? I believe it is. Religion is about us and what we do to gain God's favor and make spiritual progress. It focuses on doing better to be better.

Grace takes a totally opposite approach. Grace assures us that it isn't about you and me and what we do to improve ourselves for God. It never has been and never will be. It's about Him and His ridiculous, irrational, excessive, loving grace. The self-righteous crowd might as well calm down. Jesus is Jesus, and He's not going to change to fit their expectations or ours. Thank God.

39

Forgiving Ourselves

*Be kind to one another, tender-hearted, forgiving each
other, just as God in Christ also has forgiven you.*

—Ephesians 4:32

I know God has forgiven me, but I just can't forgive myself," someone recently said to me. He had just described a recent time in his life
when he had repeatedly made the choice to commit the same sin again
and again. He had finally reached the place where he couldn't stand the
thought of living like that anymore. So he cried out to his Deliverer, and
the cycle of sin was broken.

The foolish behavior was now a thing of the past, but he couldn't
disconnect from it mentally and emotionally. A sense of guilt and self-
condemnation was draining him of his energy, enthusiasm, and joy.
Though he wasn't committing the sin anymore, he was still as miserable
as he had been when he was.

"So you do believe that God has forgiven you?" I asked.

"Yes," he answered, "but I can't forgive myself for what I've done. I've
been a Christian long enough to know better."

After we had talked awhile and nothing I said seemed to be sinking in,
I finally asked him, "Do you think you're better than God?"

"What do you mean?" he asked.

"I mean that if the blood of Christ is sufficient for God to look at you
and say, 'Forgiven,' what will it take for you to forgive yourself? If the
death of Jesus Christ on the cross for this sin you committed isn't enough

for you, what will it take? You've set a standard for yourself that is obviously higher than the one God has set."

"I guess that's true," he mumbled.

But I could tell he wasn't buying it. He seemed to want to hang on to his guilt. Have you ever been at that place in your life? I have—and though it might sound strange, that kind of attitude is a serious insult to the finished work of Christ. In fact, I'm not so sure it doesn't border on blasphemy.

Paul taught us to forgive each other as Christ has forgiven us. It isn't uncommon that when a person has trouble forgiving others or himself, the problem is a deficiency in totally understanding God's forgiveness toward us. If we don't both know and feel that we are truly forgiven by God, it makes it hard to extend forgiveness. How can we give something we aren't sure we even possess? If you don't know that God has completely let go of anything He had against you, you may have a problem letting yourself go free from unforgiveness.

If you don't forgive yourself for the wrong things you've done, you will always carry within you a discordant counterpoint that muddies the melody of grace in your life. The discord may even be unconscious, but it still will affect how you relate to yourself. And you do relate to yourself in a particular way. Here's how.

All of us have an "internal voice" that speaks to us. It's the involuntary thoughts that go through our minds every moment of every day. If you're holding onto unforgiveness toward yourself, the voice will often be negative, reminding you of your flaws, failures, and other negative things it can dredge up against you.

The way to silence that voice is to appropriate God's forgiveness toward you and then release yourself from any guilt or shame you may still hold onto about anything you think you've done wrong. It is only through forgiveness that the accusing voice will be silenced. When you believe you are totally forgiven, there will be no grounds for further self-condemnation or judgment.

When Jesus declared from the cross, "It is finished," He meant it. All your sins—past, present, and future—have been dealt with completely. "He canceled the record [the Law] that contained the charges against us.

He took it and destroyed it by nailing it to Christ's cross" (Colossians 2:14 NLT).

Either the cross was enough to deal with your sins, or else Christianity is a sham. When we hold onto our sins and nurture self-loathing, we're actually indicating that the blood of Christ isn't enough. We, in essence, are saying, "Yes, Jesus. I know You died for me, but I have to add my part too." To try to have any part in divine forgiveness is self-idolatry because it suggests that we have to have a part in dealing with our sins. It implies that Jesus didn't really take all our sins into Himself.

Choose at this moment to inwardly speak the truth to yourself. Let go of the lies that have held your self-awareness back and kept you from thinking the best about yourself, seeing yourself as your Father sees you. Let yourself off the hook by affirming that not only has God forgiven you but also that you, right here and now, are releasing yourself from the ever-present sense of deficiency caused by not extending grace to yourself.

Have you ever noticed your inclination to show more grace to others than you do to yourself? It isn't uncommon for people to be harder on themselves than they are on others, but that isn't healthy or biblical. The Bible says we are to love others as we love ourselves. How can you love others, forgiving them for their wrongs, until you have first come to the place where you relate to yourself in that way? It isn't possible. It's time to exercise faith and set aside the wrong thinking that has influenced you.

Your self-condemnation, criticism, and negative "internal voice" are counterproductive. Forgive yourself by submitting yourself to the complete forgiveness that is already yours in Christ. The only thing you need to do is to receive it, believing it's true. And it is, because God has said so. Don't live in the prison of self-condemnation another day. Forgive yourself. Don't wait another hour.

40

Getting Along with Other People

*If it is possible, as far as it depends on
you, live at peace with everyone.*

—ROMANS 12:18 NIV

The newspaper report described how a 53-year-old man had been charged with assault after a 15-minute brawl at the rural Full Gospel Holiness Church. The brawl began when one person wanted to occupy a spot on the back pew, which was occupied, as usual, by a church regular. The article went on to say that the church minister's son suffered a bite to the neck that required 31 stitches.

You can't make this stuff up. It's a true story. Hard to believe, but true.

While it is unlikely you've ever been in a brawl inside a church building, the chances are that there is at least one other person in your life with whom you tend to have problems. How can we get along with people with whom it is often hard to live peaceably?

The apostle Paul had a word on the matter that can help immeasurably. He wrote, "From now on we recognize no one according to the flesh" (2 Corinthians 5:16). Then in the next verse he said, "If anyone is in Christ, he is a new creature."

What does this have to do with getting along with people? It has to do with the way we choose to relate to them. To know somebody after the flesh is to determine their identity based on superficial, earthly things—such as their behavior, their position...things like that.

Paul said that he chose not to know people within that context. Instead, he points to the fact that, in Christ, we are new creatures. When we choose by faith to look past the human flaws in other people and see Jesus in them, it becomes much easier to "be at peace with them." We can't control how others act, but we can determine how we will respond to them.

Jesus described how we are to relate to others, saying,

> You have heard that it was said, "You shall love your neighbor and hate your enemy." But I say to you, Love your enemies and pray for those who persecute you, so that you may be sons of your Father who is in heaven. For he makes his sun rise on the evil and on the good, and sends rain on the just and on the unjust. For if you love those who love you, what reward do you have? Do not even the tax collectors do the same? And if you greet only your brothers, what more are you doing than others? Do not even the Gentiles do the same? You therefore must be perfect, as your heavenly Father is perfect (Matthew 5:43-48 ESV).

The words of Jesus sounded just as strange to those who heard Him speak them in His own day as they sound to us today. How are we to love our enemies?

It is by recognizing that God loves them. He blesses them just as He blesses you. Jesus then goes on to tell us something that seems impossible at first glance. He says, "You therefore must be perfect, as your heavenly Father is perfect." How can any of us possibly do such a thing? The answer isn't complicated. We execute perfection in our love for others by resting in His perfect love.

We don't muster up love from within ourselves apart from Him. To the contrary, it is His love that we express to others, even those we would otherwise find hard to love. First John 4:7 says, "Beloved, let us love one another, for love is from God, and whoever loves has been born of God and knows God" (ESV). The answer becomes clear in this verse. We don't love those who are difficult by reaching into our own abilities. We simply become channels of God's love. Love is from Him. We are conduits through which that love flows.

When you find it hard to get along with somebody, start by praying a quick prayer for the person. Ask Jesus to express love to them through you. When we react negatively to difficult people, we have allowed them to control us. Why let somebody else get you in a bad mood? You can choose to express love to them and not allow the circumstance to rob you of your own joy.

Then, remember that the troublesome person may have some kind of conflict going on inside themselves. A salesclerk in a store once acted very rudely to me. My first impulse was to react the same way, but instead I paused, looked at her, and sincerely asked, "Are you having a bad day?"

To my amazement, she began to pour out the personal things that were troubling her. I was so glad that I hadn't acted on my first impulse. Her demeanor had instantly softened when I had asked that question. It was one of those "God-moments" when He allowed me to see the importance of responding in love and not reacting impulsively.

Finally, recognize that the problem may be within you and not within the other person. There have been times I've found myself repeatedly irritated by other people before it finally dawned on me: They aren't doing anything wrong. I'm just in a bad mood today! Maybe whatever irritates you in another person isn't a bad quality. Maybe you're just in a bad mood yourself.

Paul determined to look beyond human characteristics and see Jesus in others. Mother Teresa was once asked about her work with lepers, "Do you imagine that it is Jesus ministering to them when you serve them?" "No," she answered. "When I look at them, I see the face of Jesus."

There's the key—seeing Jesus in others. Look beyond the misbehavior and see Jesus in the face of those you meet. As much as it is possible, live at peace. That choice expresses the life of Christ.

By the way, if anybody ever wants to take your regular seat in church, especially if it is on the back row—let them.

41

Sometimes God Works in Not-So-Mysterious Ways

Every good thing given and every perfect gift is from above, coming down from the Father of lights, with whom there is no variation or shifting shadow.

—James 1:17

Over three decades ago, I was a struggling pastor in a small country church, barely earning enough income to keep food on the table and pay my bills. My four children were all still very young.

One day my daughter, Amy, came in and asked me if we could go to Disney World. Immediately the others chimed in too. I told them we didn't have the money to go, but we would pray and ask the Lord to make a way for us to go sometime. I knew that for our family to be able to do this would take about $500, which seemed like a fortune to me.

The children took my advice, however. Immediately, they all started praying for that desire at every occasion. Every night when our family prayed together they would each ask, "Lord, please give us money so we can go to Disney World." Night after night, their prayer was the same. "Give us the money to go to Disney World." At mealtime, the prayer from them was "Thank You for this food, and please give us the money to go to Disney World." Nobody could have prayed with more consistency and sincerity than my children.

As summer came and the weeks passed, it began to be apparent to me that we weren't going to be able to take that trip despite all the kids' prayers. Melanie and I tried to distract them from the idea by doing other things with them, but they kept praying. I hated to see their prayer go unanswered, but there was nothing I could do. I began to cringe every time one of them prayed about Disney World. While I appreciated their childlike faith, I reasoned that they didn't understand the reality of being in a situation where there were more expenses than income. I wished they'd just forget about it—but it didn't happen.

One day there was a knock at the door. When I answered, there stood two friends from our church congregation. I invited the two men in and we sat down in the living room. Suddenly, Jim stood up, walked over to where I sat, and dropped $500 in my lap. "Take your kids to Disney World," he said matter-of-factly.

"What made you do this?" I asked in disbelief. "Well," Jim answered, "it's just something Marjorie and I and Clarence and Shirley want to do." I was amazed.

That afternoon I went to the bank and exchanged the big bills for one-dollar bills. That night before we prayed, I took out the cash and began to throw it up in the air around my children. "Look!" I said to them. "The Lord answered our prayers!" We were all thrilled, and we did indeed take that trip to Disney World.

An amazing answer to prayer, don't you think?

Well, here's, as they say, "the rest of the story." Later we learned that our daughter, Amy, was in the Sunday-school class taught by one of the wives of these two men. And every week when the children prayed in Sunday school, Amy would pray aloud, "Lord, please give us the money to go to Disney World!"

Shirley had heard that prayer week after week and had told Jim's wife, Marjorie. The women had talked to their husbands. And the result was $500 in my lap a few days later.

When I learned what had happened I was embarrassed at first, but it didn't take more than a few moments for me to sense the Lord gently reminding me not to discount the way He had answered the prayer of young children who had put their request before Him in simple faith. I almost missed seeing the reality that a prayer had been answered, regardless of how it had come to happen.

God once told Isaiah, "My thoughts are not your thoughts, nor are your ways My ways." When we pray, it may be our inclination sometimes to imagine how God is going to answer that prayer, but He is much more creative than we can imagine.

As you pray about needs in your own life, don't make the mistake of assuming how the prayer will be answered. Maybe your Father will answer your prayer in a way you aren't expecting. However the answer comes, thank Him for it. We dishonor Him when we explain away what He has done by talking or acting as if it just happened to work out that way.

One time when my car wasn't running right, a mechanic told me I needed a new timing belt, an expense that I couldn't afford at the time. I prayed and asked how I would be able to pay for such a costly repair. I thought God needed to give me cash, and soon!

Shortly afterward, somebody suggested I take the car to his mechanic so I did. When he looked at it, he concluded the problem could be repaired without having to replace the timing belt. The savings were substantial. God had answered my prayer, just not in the way I'd expected.

When a need in your life is met, it's important to recognize that however it may have happened, the Ultimate Giver is the One who has provided. When you pray to get well and do, thank God for it. When you pray for guidance and find the way, recognize that it was Him. When a financial need is met, recognize where the provision came from.

Whatever it is you need and then receive, don't fail to see its real source. What things can you recall even now that showed God's favor toward you in ways that might have been explained away? Remember, your Father cares about your needs. Sometimes He answers your prayers in clearly seen ways. At other times, His answer comes in such a way that it could be imperceptible if you aren't paying attention. Return to childlike faith and know that He cares about every detail of your life.

42

Who Is Qualified?

He has made us competent as ministers of a new
covenant—not of the letter but of the Spirit;
for the letter kills, but the Spirit gives life.

—2 Corinthians 3:6 niv

Do you ever wonder if you're really qualified to be somebody whose life God can work through? Doubting your eligibility to be a vessel in His hands may look like humility at first glance, but it is really a subtle tool of the enemy to keep you from recognizing your potential in His kingdom.

It is thrilling to discover from the Bible the kind of people God will take and work through to accomplish His purposes. Those listed as heroes of the faith in Hebrews 11 were, for the most part, definitely not people most of us would have chosen as role models. Or, if we had decided to list their names, at least we would have left out some of the gory details of the inconsistent and wrong behavior that marked their lives at times.

There are the exceptions, such as Abel, Enoch, Samuel, and a few others with whom we would be hard-pressed to find much fault. Then there are the others—the majority, in fact—whose lifestyles often looked more like a dirty movie than the biography of a Bible character. Noah is listed as a person of great faith, yet the man was found lying in a drunken stupor no sooner than the ground was dry enough for him to fall down on. In Genesis 8:20, he is seen building an altar shortly after he stepped out of the ark. Then, in Genesis 9:21, he is seen drunk and naked, and seemingly (according to many Bible scholars) doing some things that would make the average churchgoer cringe to even think about.

Mentioned next in the lineup is Abraham, who is commended so strongly in Hebrews 11 that it seems as if the Holy Spirit has completely forgotten that He had already given us the lowdown on the man in the book of Genesis. Abraham took a concubine named Hagar to try to produce the son God had promised. Nobody would argue that what he did wasn't wrong, but most people who know their own propensity toward doubting God at times can let that one slide. But what about Genesis 12, where he told Sarah to tell everybody she was his sister when they arrived in Egypt? He let her be "taken into Pharaoh's house" to save himself (Genesis 12:11-15). He was willing to give her to someone else sexually because he was afraid!

Most people wouldn't recommend Abraham as "Husband of the Year," but God lists him as a man of great faith. Apparently God more readily looks past behavior and into the heart than most of us can imagine or are willing to practice ourselves.

In Hebrews 11:32, the writer said that time wouldn't permit him to mention all the heroes of faith. Read the chapter and consider the lives of those mentioned. There is Isaac, who committed the same sin as his father (Genesis 26:6-9). Then there is Jacob, who until this day is remembered as sneaky and conniving for much of his lifetime. Moses is mentioned, despite the fact that he once killed a man (Exodus 2:11-12). Samson and David are both on the list, even though both of them had adulterous affairs that are remembered to this day. Hebrews 11:31 plainly refers to Rahab as "Rahab the harlot."

How does it cause you to feel to think that God used people who behaved like that? I hope it causes you to be encouraged. Why would He use people who had been cowards, perverts, murderers, adulterers, and harlots? It is because of grace! Let the record show that much of their misbehavior came after they had come to know and follow God. Our tendency is to often try to get past the misbehavior of people by saying, "Well, they weren't believers then." But these in Hebrews 11 were believers when they misbehaved in such obvious ways.

Does grace mean that God is soft on our sin? Sometimes people accuse those who teach grace of that. God is not soft on sin, nor am I advocating that we should act like sin doesn't matter. It was sin that put Jesus on the cross, so we aren't being soft in our attitude toward sin. However, we should be soft on people! That includes you. Don't think for a moment that God can't use your life because of sins you have committed since you became a Christian. You've failed? Welcome to the club. Read Hebrews 11 to learn the names of our charter members. Our club has a rich heritage, doesn't it? Then after you have read their names and remembered their sins, thank God that He has forgiven yours. If He could use only people who never sinned, He wouldn't have anybody in this world through whom He could work.

God's grace is bigger than your biggest mistakes, most foolish choices, and most sinful actions. Where sin abounds, grace still abounds much more. Despite your sins—even if they happened after you became a Christian—you can be a faith superstar. By His grace, He has made you competent to serve Him and bless others. Put the past behind. When you fall, get up. Keep your eyes on Jesus. Move forward. And all along the way, thank God for His grace!

43

Hearing God's Voice

*My sheep hear My voice, and I know
them, and they follow Me.*

—JOHN 10:27

In his book *Without Feathers*, Woody Allen offers a spoof of the biblical
story of Abraham and Isaac. As Allen tells the story, Abraham is report-
ing to Sarah and Isaac about how God has instructed him to offer Isaac
as a sacrifice. While the following dialogue contains elements of humor,
seriously, it isn't so far removed from the way some people think God has
to speak to them.

> And Abraham awoke in the middle of the night and said to
> his only son, Isaac, "I have had a dream where the voice of the
> LORD sayeth that I must sacrifice my only son, so put your
> pants on." And Isaac trembled and said, "So what did you say?
> I mean when he brought this whole thing up?"
>
> "What am I going to say?" Abraham said. "I'm standing
> there at two a.m. in my underwear with the Creator of the
> Universe. Should I argue?"
>
> "Well, did he say why he wants me sacrificed?" Isaac asked
> his father.
>
> But Abraham said, "The faithful do not question. Now
> let's go because I have a heavy day tomorrow."
>
> And Sarah…said, "How doth thou know it was the
> Lord?"…

> And Abraham answered, "Because I know it was the Lord.
> It was a deep, resonant voice, well modulated, and nobody in
> the desert can get a rumble in it like that."*

Do you hear the voice of God as He speaks to you? Woody Allen's humorous spoof isn't that far removed from the way some people think God has to speak. They expect something very different from the way He actually communicates with us.

If we want to hear the voice of God, we need to learn to recognize His voice. Don't wait for a deep, resonant voice, well-modulated. Your God knows the language you speak, and He knows how to speak to you in a way you are most likely to recognize.

If you want to hear God's voice, start by looking within yourself to the indwelling Christ. Jesus isn't a distant deity whom you must reach in a place far outside yourself. Instead, look inward where He resides within you. Here is an exercise I've often used with people that has helped many:

Imagine Jesus walking into the room where you are right now. He walks across to you and stands directly in front of you. He reaches out and puts His arms around you and pulls you close to Himself to hug you.

Relax. Still your busy mind. Just rest in His embrace. He gently presses His face against your own and quietly whispers in your ear, "I love you so much. Do you know how proud I am of you? I love you more than you can possibly know. Sh-h-h. Be still and know that I love you."

Listen to Him. Wait until you sense an inner calmness. Ask Him to speak a personal word, just to you. Listen. Do you hear His voice? Linger here, in this still, quiet place, and allow Him to express His love. Wait... until you know it is appropriate to resume normal activity. Revel in His love. Don't rush.

Are you uncomfortable with an exercise like this? Is there anything unbiblical about what I have described? Is there anything untrue about the above scenario? Jesus does love you just as I have described. He does embrace you in His arms and long to express His love to you in meaningful

---

* Woody Allen, "The Scrolls," in *Without Feathers* (New York: Ballantine Books, 1986), p. 26.

ways. I haven't asked you to pretend anything, but rather by faith to see in your mind's eye something that is real.

Don't be uncomfortable with such intimacy. Sometimes men protest that such an exercise feels unnatural to them. They are correct. It is unnatural. It is supernatural. Relax. This isn't an issue about gender. It is a matter of learning to relax in your loving Father's embrace the way you always longed to with your earthly father when you were a young boy. Despite the messages of contemporary culture, men don't outgrow the need for affection. If it is uncomfortable, practice the awareness of His affectionate presence until it becomes comfortable.

If you don't see yourself as affectionate, ask the Holy Spirit to renew your mind to the fact that your heavenly Father is an affectionate Person. He wants to pour out His affection on you. Once you have learned to receive it from Him, you will be encouraged to discover how much easier it is for you to give it to others who have needed your affection for so long.

Jesus said that you are one of His sheep. You can be assured that He speaks to you every day. The key that unlocks our ability to hear Him is to want to hear His voice and to keep our ears open, knowing He can speak to us in many different ways and through many different means.

To hear our God speak also necessitates that we open our hearts and revel in the awareness of His tender love. It is from hearing His voice that we will discover how all the activity of our lives can be carried out in the awareness of His supernatural love—the love enjoyed by those who learn to hear Him as He passionately declares His love for us.

God isn't a religious deity who stands aloof from you and who can't be experienced within the context of your normal life. He is with you every moment, in every environment where you find yourself. Ask Him to open your ears so you can hear Him speak. When He does speak, don't rationalize it away as if nothing real has happened. Instead, thank Him and keep listening.

44

Holy Hugs

*Beloved, let us love one another, for love is from God; and
everyone who loves is born of God and knows God.*

1 JOHN 4:7

Jacob is a young man whose life is a clear demonstration of divine grace. I heard him share his story with his church family a few years ago when he was just 18 years old. He shared truths about the comfort of God during the trials of life, a topic circumstances have made him highly qualified to speak about.

When Jake was born, it soon became apparent that his parents would not be able to care for him in the way all babies need. Because of this, his dad's mother, a Christian, brought him into her home when he was an infant.

"One day when I was about five," he explained, "I learned that my mother had taken her own mother's life earlier that week." As Jake shared the horror he had felt when he learned that his own mother had murdered his grandmother, many who listened wiped tears of compassion from their eyes.

"Years later," he continued, "I opened a letter one day. It was from my mother, who is in prison. I soon learned that it had been addressed to my sister, not me. The letter said, 'You were conceived in love, but Jacob was not.' You can imagine how that would make you feel."

Jake then described how he had first come to attend the church where he was speaking. He talked about how he had met Jesus Christ there and had come to understand His love. "All I had to do was accept His comfort and His love," he explained. "Maybe you need God's comfort in your own life," he concluded. "He's there, waiting for you to trust Him."

A story this intense, told by an 18-year-old, touched the whole congregation. When the service was over, teary-eyed people crowded around Jake. They each hugged him and spoke words of appreciation and affirmation to him. It was Love personified in the body of Christ, a divine response through the corporate action of God's church.

As my wife, Melanie, and I awaited our chance to speak to him, his grandmother jokingly commented, "I think he comes here for the hugs." As we drove back home later, I commented to Melanie that Jake's grandmother's observation—"He comes here for the hugs"—was a profound commentary on the church.

What a tribute to God's church in general and that church in particular! Is there any other place in the world where a boy who missed the parental hugs necessary to nurture life could find such an outpouring of love? The ministry of hugs—what an expression of Jesus in action!

I believe the Father's heart can be seen in a hug. It may be that there is a supernatural exchange in a hug between two people that defies explanation. A holy hug somehow brings God's heart right out into the open.

When the apostle Paul once preached until midnight in one church, a young man sitting on a window ledge fell asleep and fell out the window. Rushing out to where he lay below, the Bible says that "Paul...threw himself on him and *hugged* him. 'Don't worry,' he said, 'he is still alive!'" (Acts 20:10 GNT). Hugging people back to health—that was Paul's style. In Luke 15:20, when the prodigal son came home, his dad "ran to his son, embraced him, and kissed him" (NLT). A hug and kiss—that's our Father's heart.

I love the story of Jesus with His disciples in the upper room. John 13 describes the scene. Jesus is sharing final thoughts with His disciples in the last hours before He was to go to the cross. Right in the middle of this chapter, there is a verse that seems to be almost incidental. It says, "One of the disciples, the one Jesus loved dearly, was reclining against him, his head on his shoulder" (John 13:23 MSG). Why does the Bible tell the posture of one man who happened to be sitting in the room at the time?

It's because the man described there is the one who wrote that verse. John loved to refer to himself as "the one Jesus loved dearly." It seems like he was making a point—"Jesus was talking to us all, but He was *hugging me!*" A hugging Jesus—that's the One who loves you dearly too!

In Acts 10, the Bible tells the story of Peter sharing the gospel with the household of Cornelius. As the apostle told them about the loving forgiveness of God, the Bible says, "While Peter was still speaking these words, the Holy Spirit *fell upon* all those who were listening to the message" (Acts 10:44). The words "fell upon" actually mean to closely embrace somebody. As Peter preached to his hearers about God's love, God hugged them! It is the exact word used of the father of the prodigal son when he ran to him, "*fell on* his neck, and kissed him" (Luke 15:20).

A hug—is anything more powerful, more spiritual, more Godlike? It became apparent to me as I watched Jake's church family that he won't ever lack for hugs. His heavenly Father has seen to that. I watched his *Abba* hug him many times after that service through the arms of others. I couldn't resist hugging him myself, and not just because he is my nephew.

Do you want to do a Jesus thing? Find somebody today who needs a hug and give it to them. That won't be a hard task, because the truth is, we all could use a hug. Some desperately need it. A hug is the heart of God in action toward others. Go ahead. Find somebody and hug them back to health. Your Father will be proud.

45

Hurricanes and Jugglers

He said to them, "Why are you afraid?
Do you still have no faith?"

—Mark 4:40

I was in Puerto Vallarta, Mexico, where I was speaking in a local church. My friend Tim and I had shared the pulpit during the weekend and were scheduled to fly home on Monday morning.

At the end of the final church service, the pastor stood up in front of the congregation and announced he had just received a telephone call about a hurricane that was approaching the city very quickly. We were told that it would arrive between 11 and 12 the next morning.

When we left church, we saw preparations being frantically made. People were boarding up windows at home. Businesses were taping their windows and glass doors in an effort to keep them from being blown in. We heard on the radio that authorities were already evacuating people from some areas of the city. We learned that, at some point, the roads leading out of the city would even be closed in order to prevent people from trying to leave and being hurt in the process.

The adrenaline began to pump and our hearts began beating faster as we discussed what we would do. We decided to go to the airport and, while there was still time, try to either get a flight out of town or rent a car and begin driving inland.

As we made our way along the jammed road toward the airport, we inched along until we came to a stop at a red light. I looked over to the side of the road by my window and saw a young man walk out into the street. I never would have expected to see him do what he did next. He began to juggle. He had picked up five or six balls from the sidewalk and started juggling right out in the middle of the road.

It isn't uncommon to see street entertainers who work for tips in tourist places like Puerto Vallarta. But this seemed downright strange to me. Didn't he know about the coming hurricane? Didn't he sense the tension in the air as people were scurrying around trying to prepare? Was he mentally unbalanced?

Maybe he was, maybe he wasn't. I don't know. I do know that, as I thought about the incident later, my thoughts turned to Jesus when He was in a similar situation. While out in a boat with His disciples, He too was in a storm. Mark recorded it:

> As evening came, Jesus said to his disciples, "Let's cross to the other side of the lake." He was already in the boat, so they started out, leaving the crowds behind (although other boats followed). But soon a fierce storm arose. High waves began to break into the boat until it was nearly full of water. Jesus was sleeping at the back of the boat with his head on a cushion. Frantically they woke him up, shouting, "Teacher, don't you even care that we are going to drown?" When he woke up, he rebuked the wind and said to the water, "Quiet down!" Suddenly the wind stopped, and there was a great calm. And he asked them, "Why are you so afraid? Do you still not have faith in me?" And they were filled with awe and said among themselves, "Who is this man, that even the wind and waves obey him?" (Mark 4:35-41 NLT).

They were all worried sick about the situation, all except Jesus. He was asleep in the back of the boat. Finally, one of the men awakened Jesus and frantically asked, "Don't you care that we are about to perish?" I can imagine Jesus smiling, calmly patting the fearful disciple on the shoulder, then looking at the billowing waves and gently saying, "Peace, be still!" Then He looked back at the disciple, smiled, and asked, "What are you so afraid of? Where's your faith?"

Storms will arise in life. Sometimes they even become hurricanes. What are we to do? Should we just keep on juggling all the things in our lives as if nothing threatening is happening? Should we drop everything and run?

Different situations require different responses. But one thing is sure—we are to trust Jesus at all times. He is in the boat with us and, as long as that is true, we have no reason to be afraid. The tendency we have in threatening circumstances is to immediately tally our resources and begin taking precautionary steps to minimize our losses. As many people have learned about hurricanes, although taking reasonable precautions makes sense, there is nothing we can do to guarantee the outcome of the situation. There is only One who holds that kind of power in His hands, and we must entrust ourselves and all we have to Him.

Are you being threatened by circumstances right now? Don't be afraid. Jesus is in your situation with you, and He will see to it that you reach the destination He has planned for you. The same One who will see to it that you reach your destination has chartered the boat and is navigating you toward your goal. Just relax and trust Him.

Give your boat—your life—and everything in it to Him and He will show you what to do next. He loves you. He has guaranteed that you will be safely delivered home. Have faith. Jesus is in the situation with you, and that is enough.

46

Living in Freedom

It was for freedom that Christ set us free;
therefore keep standing firm and do not be
subject again to a yoke of slavery.

—Galatians 5:1

During World War II, Jonathan Wainwright was the only United States Army general to be captured. His orders from General Douglas MacArthur were, "No surrender. Fight to the end." As the conflict in the Philippines intensified, Wainwright found himself in a position that left him two options. Either die or surrender. He surrendered. He and his army were marched to Japanese ships and transferred to POW camps all over Asia. Thousands of soldiers died.

For many long months as a prisoner in a POW camp in Mongolia, Wainwright wallowed in self-condemnation for having surrendered. His body deteriorated, and he depended on a cane to move about. His emotional lows continually caused him to feel like a total failure for having given up to the enemy.

Ultimately, General MacArthur led his troops to complete victory over the Japanese throughout the Pacific. After the Japanese empire surrendered totally and MacArthur occupied Japan, POW camps all over Asia began to be liberated. Far away in Mongolia, however, the news had not reached Wainwright. He didn't know that victory belonged to America. In ignorance he continued to live like a prisoner of war.

Eventually, an Allied airplane landed near the camp where Wainwright was imprisoned. An American officer walked to the fence, saluted, and said, "General, Japan has surrendered." Having been given that information, Wainwright stood tall, limped to the commandant's office, and shoved the door open. He walked right up to his enemy's desk and announced in a calm voice, "My commander-in-chief has defeated your commander-in-chief. I am in control now. I order you to surrender!"

The Japanese commandant rose, quietly laid down his weapon, and surrendered. Without firing a shot, Wainwright took over, despite his emaciated, handicapped physical condition.

How did he do it? It's simple. The truth had set him free. Without a struggle and out of extreme weakness, he simply believed the truth and acted in the freedom of the authority that was his. When he by faith acted in authority, according to the truth he had heard, the enemy surrendered without hesitation. Wainwright was weak. We know that his victory didn't stem from his own strength. It came from the one who had gained it for him. He simply appropriated what was his.

As a believer, you may have experienced a time in your life when you were held in the custody of sin because you didn't know the truth. You were shut up in a dark place. It wasn't that freedom wasn't your birthright. It was simply that you didn't know. Or if you did, you didn't know how to walk out the freedom that was yours.

You were held as a prisoner by a performance-based pattern for life that kept you from fully enjoying the freedom available to those who understand the grace walk. Then came faith and revelation of the truth. God gave you the revelation of who you are in Him and who He is in you. By faith in His truth, the prison doors were opened! For the first time, you saw it—that you aren't a slave to sin now!

You don't have to live like a prisoner to sin anymore. Galatians 5:1 says, "It was for freedom that Christ set us free; therefore keep standing firm and do not be subject again to a yoke of slavery." Jesus Christ has set you free. "So if the Son makes you free, you will be free indeed" (John 8:36).

Paul wrote his letter to the Galatians because they were in danger of allowing themselves to be brought back under a system of religious rules. He wanted to help them avoid falling into such a trap. He wanted them to continue to experience the freedom that was rightfully theirs.

You may know people who seek to put you under religious rules. Don't allow it to happen. Your life isn't to revolve around rules. You don't need rules, because you have the life of Jesus Christ inside you; as you trust Him to be who He is, He will animate your lifestyle in such a way that your behavior will be infinitely better than just doing the right thing. Freedom in Christ doesn't just produce right behavior. It produces *righteous* behavior! Don't worry about rules. Just keep your focus on Jesus Christ. Recognize Him as your life source, and everything else will fall in line.

If you've lived in a religious, rules-keeping environment, this may not feel right to you at first. There may be some people who tell you that you can't go too far with this grace idea—but remember that grace isn't just a doctrinal viewpoint. Grace is a Person named Jesus Christ.

"The Law was given through Moses; grace and truth were realized through Jesus Christ" (John 1:17). What does that verse tell you? Who did Law (religious rules) come from? They came from Moses, the man who delivered the Old Covenant to the people of Israel. Which covenant did Jesus bring? The New Covenant! Which of these covenants is the one you are to live under? The new, of course. You do not live under a system of religious rules. You live in the covenant of grace. Jesus brought grace *and* truth. Don't let anybody tell you that you need a "balance" of grace and truth. Jesus *is* the perfect manifestation of both!

You may have concerns that your behavior will go astray, but that would be a needless worry. The Spirit of Jesus Christ within you will regulate your behavior. That's His role. Yours is simply to trust.

Maybe you feel too weak, incapable of living in freedom. Your freedom in Christ has nothing to do with the way you feel. Like Jonathan Wainwright, you may feel weak and debilitated at times, but victory is yours because of the cross. It isn't by your effort that you gain the victory that causes you to triumph. Jesus Christ has already accomplished it for you. All you need to do is simply believe and live out the truth in your daily life—that through Him you have been emancipated from the penalty and power of sin. You have been set free!

47

Rest Awhile

*He said to them, "Come away by yourselves
to a secluded place and rest a while."*

—Mark 6:31

It had been a busy ministry trip. The disciples had seen tremendous results through preaching, casting out devils, and healing. It was with great enthusiasm that "the apostles gathered around Jesus and reported to him all they had done and taught" (Mark 6:30 NIV).

What would you imagine the response of Jesus to be at a moment like that? If His response to them was consistent with the twenty-first-century discipleship practiced in many churches, He might have said, "Good job! Don't quit now! Our momentum is going, and let's keep it that way! Get out there and keep preaching it!"

That's the kind of leadership I gave as a pastor for many years. "After all," I reasoned, "the devil never takes a day off, so why should we?" That kind of thinking makes sense to a mind trapped in a religious rut, but the response of Jesus is very different. We may think that gaining momentum and maintaining it is necessary to faithfully serve Him, but He has a different perspective:

> He said to them, "Come away by yourselves to a desolate place and rest a while." For many were coming and going, and they had no leisure even to eat. And they went away in the boat to a desolate place by themselves (Mark 6:31-32 ESV).

At a time when the disciples reported on how well things were going, Jesus said, "Great! Now, rest awhile." That kind of advice doesn't typically fit the modern mindset. It just doesn't come easily for those who have heard tireless duty stressed all our lives. Something inside us causes us to feel like we're wasting time when we rest. Yet Jesus indicated to His disciples that there is a time when it is appropriate to rest.

Recently on a ministry trip, I spent some days staying alone in a cabin. I had my to-do list all ready for the week, but God wouldn't allow me to do what I thought I needed to do. In the solitude of this isolated sanctuary, one of the things I heard the gentle voice of Jesus say was, "Rest." That word is particularly hard for those of us who are type A personalities, but even if you're not, the resounding sermon of contemporary Christianity is, "Keep going. Don't stop! The end is near and there's no time to waste!"

However, the God who rested on the seventh day after the six days of work that produced everything there is says to you, "Rest." Do you hear that word resonating somewhere deep inside you? It's true that we may continuously rest inwardly, but have you considered that God may sometimes want you to slow down outwardly too?

Even under the Old Covenant, God had specific instructions for His priests about the importance of spiritual rest. Even the way they were instructed to get dressed stressed the importance of this fact, right down to their underwear. Leviticus 16:4 gave instructions about the high priest: "He shall put on the holy linen tunic, and the linen undergarments shall be next to his body, and he shall be girded with the linen sash and attired with the linen turban (these are holy garments). Then he shall bathe his body and put them on."

Note that the underwear the priests wore was to be made of linen. Why did God care what kind of material was used in making these undergarments? Why linen? Ezekiel 44:18 answers the question: "Linen turbans shall be on their heads and linen undergarments shall be on their loins; they shall not gird themselves with anything which makes them sweat."

They were not to wear anything that made them sweat! Why? It's because these Old Testament priests foreshadowed the priesthood of the New Testament. There is a general sense in which you are a priest. First Peter 2:9 says,

You are a chosen race, a royal priesthood, a holy nation, a people for God's own possession, so that you may proclaim the
excellencies of Him who has called you out of darkness into
His marvelous light.

In your role as a New Covenant priest, you are to rest in Christ every
day. It is not His intention that you should burn out in life. That brings
Him no glory. He wants you to know the spiritual rest that will enable
you to burn on, not burn out.

Spiritual rest becomes impossible when a person reaches the place
where there is very little physical rest in his life. The greatest and maybe
most difficult obedience some of us need in response to Christ is to slow
down. If the very idea provokes mental objections within you, this may
be a good indicator that this truth is particularly applicable to you. The
things you spend your time doing will still be there after you're done resting. The world system won't fail if you take a break in order to be refreshed
and renewed.

Take a day off and spend it with your children. Visit a friend who
lives out of town. Go on a date with your spouse. Or just get alone for a
while. It may surprise you to hear the exciting things God has been waiting to tell you.

I realize that this kind of encouragement runs the risk of being labeled
"passivity" by critics of the message of God's grace, but the reality is that
most of us are in no immediate danger of becoming passive. To the contrary, we tend to wear ourselves out "for Jesus," something He never asked
us to do.

Aren't we to serve with zeal? Isn't a strong work ethic important? The
answer is obvious, but there are times too when Jesus is saying to you,
"Come away and rest awhile." Is that something you sense Him showing you to do?

48

Holy Work

Whatever you do in word or deed, do all in the name of the Lord Jesus, giving thanks through Him to God the Father.

—COLOSSIANS 3:17

I'm thinking of entering professional ministry," a young man said to me. "What do you want to do?" I asked him.

"I'm not sure," he replied, "but I want to do something in ministry full-time. I want God to use my life and don't see much opportunity for that in my work."

I didn't get into a lengthy discussion with him since his remark was made casually in passing. It did remind me again, though, of the deception that so many people have fallen for in regard to their work. Like this young man, they think that the routine work in their job isn't that spiritual, compared to the work of those who are pastors, missionaries, and so on.

This common viewpoint is a ploy of the enemy to dilute the effectiveness of Christ expressing His life through our lives. The truth is that your profession, no matter what it may be, is holy. There is no dualistic world where some things are spiritual and some aren't. Whether you are a teacher, a doctor, a clerk, a salesman—it makes no difference. Your work is holy because of who you are. *You* are holy, and as you express Christ's life, whatever you do is holy.

The word *holy* means "set apart." One of the greatest deceptions that has ever slipped into our minds is the idea that there is a difference between secular and sacred. In Jesus Christ, everything is sacred. The word *sacred* comes from the Latin *sacer*, which has basically the same meaning as our modern word: something that is dedicated or set apart—not common or everyday—because of its association with the Divine.

You have become one with God through Jesus Christ. Everything in your life is intimately associated with Him through your union to Him, thus making it sacred. Because Christ lives in you, you can trust Him to ensure that all that you do is *sanctified* (made holy) when He is the One doing the work through you. Nothing is secular (common) to you because you are "uncommon"—not common—yourself. You are defined by the fact that Divine Life has joined Himself together with you. You aren't God, but God is in you and has become inseparably joined to you.

When Moses approached the burning bush on Mount Sinai, God told him, "Remove your sandals from your feet, for the place on which you are standing is holy ground" (Exodus 3:5). The ground where Moses stood beside the burning bush was holy because God was there.

The utensils used in the temple were holy because they were set apart to be used in service to Him. It is God's presence that makes anything holy, and that includes your work. Your professional career is the context within which you have been placed to express Christ's life each day. Consequently, your work is a holy endeavor.

The apostle Paul wrote, "Don't just do what you have to do to get by, but work heartily, as Christ's servants doing what God wants you to do" (Ephesians 6:6 MSG). When a pastor preaches or a missionary evangelizes or a seminary professor teaches, each activity is holy work. However, it is equally holy when a lawyer tries a case, or a salesman makes a sale, or a long-haul driver drives his truck. It's all holy because the Christ who indwells you has sanctified it. So, whatever you do, see it as a ministry to your heavenly Father!

In *The Practice of the Presence of God,* the monk Brother Lawrence wrote,

> The time of business does not with me differ from the time of prayer, and in the noise and clatter of my kitchen, while several persons are at the same time calling for different things, I

possess God in as great tranquility as if I were upon my knees
at the blessed sacrament.

Whether it is washing dishes or taking communion, it is all holy to the
one whose life is Jesus Christ.

Don't view your work as secular. See it for what it is—a holy expression of Christ's life within you in the marketplace. To understand your
responsibilities this way will elevate them to their rightful place as a vehi-
cle through which you may glorify God.

To disassociate your activity at work from Jesus Christ is to compart-
mentalize your actions in a way that is totally unbiblical and is an insult
to the Christ who lives in you. On the pie-scale of life, He isn't one piece
of the pie, not even the biggest piece. He is the crust that holds everything else together.

You live in union with God. The word *enthusiasm* comes from two
Greek words, *en* and *theos* ("in" and "God"). In years past, to use the word
enthusiastic was like using the word *blessed* or *godly*. It was universally rec-
ognized to be a word with sacred connotation. As time has passed, the
meaning of the word has been diluted, and it has now become associated
with being excited, but for centuries people knew its real meaning: that
a person was "in God." So, to be *enthusiastic* is to be united with Deity.

This word describes you and all you do. He lives in you and will never
leave you (Ezekiel 36:27; John 20:22; Hebrews 13:5). No wonder the
apostle Paul said, "I can do all things through Him who strengthens me."

Live out this day in faith that Jesus Christ will express His life through
you as you go about your daily duties. Ask Him to renew your mind in
such a way that you never again see any activity of your life as any less holy
than another. Know that He is your life when you are at work as well as
at any other place or time. Claim the portion of your time each day that
you spend at work as His time and as a divine opportunity for Him to be
who He is in you and through you…as you work with true enthusiasm.

49

Accepting Divine Forgiveness

He made you alive together with Him, having
forgiven us all our transgressions.

—COLOSSIANS 2:13

In Victor Hugo's novel *Les Miserables*, Jean Valjean, the main character, spends the night in the home of the Bishop of Digne. Despite the generosity of the bishop toward him, Valjean rises during the night and takes valuable silver from a cabinet. Hearing the noise, the bishop awakens and walks into the room, where he sees Valjean stealing his belongings. Valjean knocks him to the ground and flees.

Later in the day, the police arrive at the rectory with Valjean in handcuffs. "He claims that you gave him the silver," one policeman scoffs. "Yes, of course I gave him the silverware," replies the priest. "Valjean, why didn't you take the candlesticks too? They are worth at least two thousand francs." Turning to his maid, the bishop orders, "Go and fetch the candlesticks. And offer these men some wine. They must be thirsty."

Left alone together, the bishop grasps Valjean by the shoulders and looks deeply into his eyes. Valjean is confused. Speaking softly, with restrained emotion, he asks, "Why are you doing this?"

The bishop answers with passion, "Jean Valjean, my brother, you no longer belong to evil. With this silver I've bought your soul. I've ransomed you from fear and hatred and now I give you back to God." With tear-filled eyes and an expression of disbelief, Valjean stands before the priest, speechless.

Forgiveness. It's a troubling concept to the morality police of this world. In the callous world of morality, meticulous records are kept that clearly reflect the debt everyone owes. But in the land of divine mercy, moral accounting is exiled to nothingness, the books are burned, and record-keeping is declared taboo.

God wants you to live without self-consciousness about anything you've done that was a dishonor to Him. He has taken the dishonor of your sin upon Himself, and it is no longer yours to bear. To wallow in ongoing remorse about sin is to express the worst sort of insult toward the One who has removed your sins and forgiven you for having ever committed them in the first place.

To paraphrase the words of the priest to Jean Valjean, Jesus has declared to you, "You no longer belong to evil. With My blood I've bought your soul. I've ransomed you from fear and hatred and have given you back to God."

Like Jean Valjean, you may stand speechless in total awe. The news of the gospel of grace may seem almost too good to be true...but believe it. Don't express contempt for the crucifixion of Jesus by insisting on carrying the shame of sins you have committed. Don't despise what He has done for you by refusing to gladly accept the forgiveness He has given. Affirm the reality that your sins are gone, never to be brought up again.

Live in the joyful freedom that can only be known by those who have embraced their forgiveness. Don't listen to even a whisper of self-condemnation that may try to find a place in your thoughts. Reject it immediately by thanking God that what He accomplished at the cross on your behalf is indeed sufficient.

50

Surviving the Storms

*The LORD hath his way in the whirlwind and in
the storm, and the clouds are the dust of his feet.*

—NAHUM 1:3 KJV

The boat was heeling over until water rushed over the rail. I braced myself to capsize at any second as the howling wind and rain beat into my face. Visions from the movie *White Squall* (in which almost everybody drowned in a storm at sea) ran through my mind. I wasn't nervous. I had passed that state ten minutes ago. I was afraid.

The incident happened years ago when Melanie and I were taking sailing lessons. We were in the middle of Sir Francis Drake Channel in the British Virgin Islands, when our instructor pointed toward the horizon and said, "See that squall in the distance?" "Yes," we answered, expecting him to tell us how we would sail around it.

"We're going to sail right into the middle of it," he said. "Take compass bearings, because you won't be able to see land when we reach the middle of it." I assumed he knew what he was doing. We soon learned that his purpose was to teach us how to maneuver the boat in adverse conditions so we would be prepared in the event that someone ever fell overboard.

"There's no better place to do a man-overboard drill than in a storm. That's where people are most likely to fall off," he explained. *That makes sense*, I thought. Well, it only made sense until we sailed into the storm. I wasn't prepared for its intensity.

Our instructor had thrown the life preserver overboard several times and we had rehearsed using only the sail to make a sudden stop and turn around to retrieve it, as we would do if a person were in the water. Things had gone fairly smoothly the first few times. But this last time, in the squall, was different. As I trimmed the sail to bring it closer to the center of the boat, Melanie began to turn the boat to make our tack.

Suddenly, in one quick instant, the wind caught the sail and the boat heeled over so the mast almost touched the water. That's when the panic hit me. It was at that point I braced myself to capsize. I didn't know what mistake we had made, but I thought it was a big one.

Instantly, I turned to look to our instructor for help. I saw him standing there—calmly. He had one foot on the rail where water was rushing over into the boat and the other on the deck. And in the midst of all this, there was an expression of perfect calm on his face.

I immediately thought to myself, *Things must be okay. He understands sailing better than us and he is perfectly calm.* I held on, the boat soon righted herself, and everything was fine.

When the situation was all over, I remarked to our instructor, "You seemed calm through the whole ordeal. I was scared to death until I saw your expression. Then I assumed everything must be okay."

"I knew the boat would turn up into the wind and everything would be alright," he answered. "That's why I wasn't worried."

I thought about what he said later and realized that life is a lot like what we experienced on the boat that day. Sometimes it's smooth sailing—when suddenly we find ourselves in a storm. We may be doing our best to navigate through it, when a gust of adversity blows in and threatens to capsize everything we hold dear.

What do we do in those moments? We turn our attention to Jesus. We intentionally look into His face, and when we do, we will see the same expression I saw on our instructor's face that day at sea—one of complete peace and calm.

What is the answer during the storms of life? It all comes back down to the foundational truth of the first four words of the Bible. "In the beginning God," says Genesis 1:1. The word "God" in the verse is the Hebrew name *Elohiym*. The word is plural and means "rulers, judges, divine ones." The word points to the Father, Son, and Holy Spirit.

During the difficult days of your life, remember that there is an Eternal Godhead who sits on high and reigns over the affairs of this world. In the beginning, God. In the end, God. In the meantime, God.

If our God is loving, as we have always professed Him to be (and He is); if He is all-powerful, as we have always professed Him to be (and He is); then you can look to Him when it seems like your existence as you know it is about to go under, knowing that whatever might happen in your life is okay. Not a sparrow falls to the ground without His knowledge. So you can be sure that you have nothing to fear.

Feelings rise and fall based on external stimuli. Faith remains steadfast, based on the eternal goodness of power of the One who holds us in His hand. So when you're scared, look to Him. When you're confused, look to Him. When life makes no sense and you don't know what to do, look to Him. You will see calmness in His face that will calm your troubled heart.

His way, His path, is in whirling winds and storms, and the clouds are the dust of His feet (Nahum 1:3). You aren't going to drown. The Captain of your salvation is in control of your destiny—He will see to it that you arrive safely at the destination He has planned for you. Don't watch the waves. Watch Him and know that regardless of anything you can see, everything is going to be okay.

51

Let's Dance

How beautiful you are, my darling,
how beautiful you are!

—Song of Solomon 1:15

He entered into the room, which was filled with noise and activity. There was music, laughter, and talking. His eyes scanned the room, searching for that one whose very face caused his breath to quicken and his heart rate to increase. He loved her, yet it was more than that. He wanted her. He wanted her to be his, and not just tonight, but forever.

Then he saw her. Across the crowded room, she stood—as if she had been unknowingly waiting for him all her life. She was beautiful. No, not beautiful. She was stunning. *God, I must have her!* he thought, every fiber of his being resonating. *I want to spend my life with her. I want to love her and cherish her and hold her. I want to take care of her and spoil her.*

He walked across the room, never taking his eyes off her for even a moment. The room was filled with people, but his eyes were on her. As he approached her, his presence caught her attention, and she looked upward into his penetrating eyes. This was the moment he had been waiting for, the time he had longed for as long as he could remember. Gently and lovingly he spoke: "Would you care to dance?"

The description I have given is a true story. The two did begin to dance that day and they have never stopped. He asked her to marry him and she said "yes." His plan is to do exactly what he intended from the beginning—to share his life with her and to love her so much that she will never regret the day she met him.

Not only is the story true, but you actually know the people involved. The one He desired to have so much is you. The Person who wanted you so badly is Jesus Christ. One day He walked into the room of this world to find you. He was captivated by you, and He determined that He would make you His own. He knew in His heart that He must have you and that He wouldn't live without you.

If you doubt my words about His love, read the following marriage proposal He wrote you. These aren't my words, but are His, copied here word for word exactly as He wrote them to you:

> How beautiful you are, my darling, how beautiful you are!…
> There is no blemish in you!…
> Arise, my darling, my beautiful one, and come along!…
> You have made my heart beat faster with a single glance
>   of your eyes…
> How delightful you are, my love, with all your charms!

This note to you is recorded in the Bible, in the Song of Solomon (Song of Solomon 1:15; 4:7; 2:13; 4:9; 7:6). This book of the Bible is a love story about you and Jesus. Its words are sometimes so graphic, so intense, that throughout church history there have been those who have argued it shouldn't even be in the Bible. However, your Divine Lover has made sure it is there. The Song of Solomon is a love poem written for you. Its eight stanzas call you beautiful no less than fifteen times!

Jesus is consumed with you. You may not feel that way about yourself, but it makes no difference. What He says is an objective fact, whether you believe it or not. If you don't believe it now, rest assured that you will believe it, because He is going to keep telling you how beautiful and precious you are to Him throughout all eternity. One day, either now or later, the reality of His words will transform you.

Do you remember the day you heard Him ask you to dance? Maybe it was in church, or perhaps it was when a friend shared his or her faith with you. Maybe it was when you were all alone and heard the voice of the Holy Spirit. Do you remember what you experienced then as He reached out to you? The bride in the Song of Solomon spoke for us all when she said, "My feelings were aroused for him" (5:4). That happened to us all when Jesus swept us off our feet and we trusted Him.

The first time you heard His invitation to dance may be a moment in time you remember well, but His desire to bring you to the Eternal Dance of the Father, Son, and Spirit has been a dream in the loving heart of God from eternity past. There has never been a moment when God's plans didn't involve creating you, courting you, caring for you, and then carrying you throughout the ages to come.

Don't think it irreverent to view Christ in a romantic way. He is the One who calls us His bride. He is the One who wrote to us in terms of passion and romance. We simply respond to Him. "We love him, because he first loved us" (1 John 4:19 KJV). We didn't initiate or set the pace for this relationship. He did. We have simply responded to His irresistible charm, affirming by faith, "My beloved is mine, and I am his" (Song of Solomon 2:16)! Like every new bride, our profession of faith in Him is nothing less than the thrilling realization that "I am my beloved's, and his desire is for me" (7:10)!

I didn't imagine the idea of the dance as a literary metaphor to describe your relationship to Him. That is how He described it. In Zephaniah 3:17, the Bible says, "He will rejoice over you with shouts of joy." *Strong's Concordance* defines the Hebrew word that is translated "rejoice" in the following way: "To spin around under the influence of a violent emotion."

One day you will meet face-to-face the One whom "having not seen, ye love" (1 Peter 1:8 KJV). You will look into the eyes that have never looked away from you even once. You will be embraced by His outstretched arms and will hear His voice audibly. I'm not sure what His first words to you will be, but it wouldn't surprise me if the first thing He says as He stares deeply into your eyes is simply, "Let's dance."

52

Dare to Live Your Dream

Delight yourself in the LORD; and He will
give you the desires of your heart.

—Psalm 37:4

I've never known what I want to do with my life," a young mother said to me after I had spoken about how to embrace the dreams God puts into our hearts. "I want to fulfill God's plan for me, but I can't figure out what it is. I don't even know what I want to do," she continued.

After asking her a few questions, I said to her, "We've just met, so I obviously don't know you. But I'd like to offer one common reason that often applies when people can't seem to identify the unique plan that God has for them. Is that okay?"

"Sure," she answered.

I continued. "A very common reason for people not being able to figure out what they want to do with their life is this: They've never given themselves the freedom to think about what they want because they've spent their whole life trying to please others."

I paused. The woman stared at me for a moment, then looked at her friend beside her with an expression of disbelief. "He hit that one on the head, didn't he?" she remarked. Her friend laughed.

It didn't take a counseling genius to figure out the problem—just 40 years of talking with thousands of people like this young woman. A great number of people have never realized God's wonderful plan for their lives because they've never allowed themselves to consider their own desires. If they don't do that, they can seldom discern God's will for themselves.

God gives you the desires of your heart. That means He is the One who places them there. But if you don't know who you are, you may spend your whole life trying to fulfill other people's plans for your life. Many a frustrated person has struggled with finding fulfillment in life by trying to be something and do something they've never been directed by God to be or do.

One aspect of God's grace is divine enablement. By His grace, God enables you to be all He has called you to be and do all He has created you to do. Remember this, however: His grace doesn't empower you to be and do what somebody else has indicated you need to do. You live in union with the Triune God of heaven. His life dwells in you and seeks to flow through you in powerful, creative expressions of love in this world.

Who He has made you to be is wonderful, so you must resolve to be that person. Any effort to be somebody else is an affront to Him because it suggests that you (or others) know better who you're supposed to be and what you're supposed to be doing.

Don't live for other people. It will wear you out. Instead, live from the union you share with your Father through Christ. Know that you are empowered by His Spirit. Then you will be free to be and do all that you were designed for. The apostle Paul once said, "I'm not trying to be a people pleaser! No, I'm trying to please God. If I were still trying to please people, I would not be Christ's servant" (Galatians 1:10 NLT).

Have you behaved like a people-pleaser? Maybe you grew up in a home where you sought to find acceptance by doing what your family expected. Maybe you learned early in life that you could make friends by conforming to what they wanted you to be. Maybe your spouse has evoked feelings in you that have caused you to think you have to meet expectations in order to be acceptable. There are many reasons why people become people-pleasers.

You will never experience the peace that comes from knowing you are fulfilling a divine plan for your life without breaking the bad habit of allowing others to dictate your decisions and actions. Begin today to stand up and do what you believe is right for you. Maybe you'll feel afraid at first, but that's okay. Do it anyway. If others criticize you, do it anyway. If you doubt yourself, trust God and do it anyway! This is your life in Christ, and only He can determine the direction of your life. So trust Him and move forward to live the dream He has placed inside you.

If you want to find fulfillment—if you want to be and do all you were created to be and do—stop trying to run the course other people set for you. Your desires count because God has placed them there.

Combine the promises of God fulfilled on your behalf in Jesus Christ with His ability to express those already fulfilled promises (in Him), and there is no reason to be anything but positive! The Bible says,

> Be strong and take courage, all you who put your hope in the
> LORD…The LORD's delight is in those…who put their hope
> in his unfailing love…Surely you have a future ahead of you;
> your hope will not be disappointed…"I know the plans I have
> for you," says the LORD. "They are plans for good and not for
> disaster, to give you a future and a hope"…There is hope for
> your future.*

Will you believe God? You have the enabling grace of the Christ within you to live a supernatural life. Will you accept and appropriate the good news and rise up in confidence? Will you lay hold of the hope—that of fulfilling the God-given dreams of your heart?

The apostle Paul did. He wrote, triumphantly, "Now glory be to God! By his mighty power at work within us, he is able to accomplish infinitely more than we would ever dare to ask or hope!" (Ephesians 3:20 NLT). "Without wavering, let us hold tightly to the hope we say we have, for God can be trusted to keep his promise" (Hebrews 10:23 NLT).

Allow Jesus to express boldness through you. Rise up and seize the day, filled with optimistic faith in the Creator, who designed your blueprint for living. Let Him live through you and watch your life start to be transformed!

---

* Respectively: Psalm 31:24 NLT; Psalm 147:11 NLT; Proverbs 23:18 NLT; Jeremiah 29:11 NLT; Jeremiah 31:17 NLT.

53

Making Our Days Count

*Teach us to number our days, that we
may gain a heart of wisdom.*

—Psalm 90:12

There is a benefit to understanding that your days are numbered. None of us are going to live forever in this world. Knowing that we have a finite number of days here can motivate us to make the time we have left really count for eternity.

If you want an eye-opening moment, check out one of numerous websites that will project your date of death based on answers you give about your present lifestyle choices. It is a shock to see your death date predicted in stark numbers by a computer. Of course, we all know that nobody can be precise in predicting when any of us will die, but the computer prediction makes a powerful point nonetheless. There is a definite day and hour when you will leave this earth-life, when the opportunities of this world will be gone. We need to redeem the time because our time here is a finite commodity.

On His last night, Jesus prayed to His Father, "I glorified You on the earth, having accomplished the work which You have given Me to do" (John 17:4). Nobody ever lived out a God-designed plan with the effectiveness Jesus Christ did. He repeatedly said that the only way He did it was by depending on God the Father to express His life through Him, the Son. Every aspect of His actions was an expression of the Father's life within Him.

It is important to consider each day the things the Father has for you to do. The grace walk is grounded in being, not doing, but that doesn't mean there is no "doing." When we understand that we live in union with God Himself, we *want* to do things that honor Him in this life! It's not a legalistic list of things we have to accomplish that motivates us, but a desire to live our lives to the fullest.

You are destined for more than to loiter on Planet Earth for 70 or 80 years, then go to heaven. This world isn't a waiting room. It is the stage upon which we participate in the expression of Divine Life in a way that is nothing short of supernatural. Your life is a unique expression of His infinite life and love.

Your life is a part of eternity's divine drama. It is the love story of Jesus Christ and you. Let others cower or kill time in the wings if that's what they choose, but don't choose that for yourself. At a deep level, you sense that you are meant to fulfill a wonderful part God has written for you. His grace empowers you to assume your role with confidence and live out your part in a way that will send ripples across His kingdom.

You can make every day count because He has already accomplished in eternity the good things you will experience in your allotted days here. Isaiah said, "Lord, You will establish peace for us, since You have also performed for us all our works" (Isaiah 26:12). Can you see that it's a done deal? All you need to do is trust Him to guide you to walk out in time what has already been done in eternity.

The apostle Paul zeros in on this aspect of our life mission in Ephesians 2:10. I love the way the verse is put in the New Living Translation: "We are God's masterpiece. He has created us anew in Christ Jesus, so that we can do the good things he planned for us long ago."

If you choose wisdom and make your days count, you will find that as Jesus lives His life through you, you will love people more. You will find yourself showing greater love to your family, to your friends, even to strangers. Jesus in you may even find people who aren't "all that lovable" on the surface and show love to them. He was often criticized for loving the wrong kind of people. Has that ever happened to you? Don't be surprised if it does when His love captivates you.

When grace fills your heart, you may discover it oozing out as love on the most unlikely people. Human love is highly discriminating, but *agape* is the unconditional love that flows right from the heart of God. As His love overflows in your life, others will find themselves receiving that love—a love that makes no sense in human terms but becomes a means of healing to them just because they have encountered you. You can leave every person you engage today in a better condition than before they encountered you just because the love of Jesus flows out of you to them.

Making our days count means voluntarily giving up control over our lives, putting that control into the hands of our loving Father. We all act like control freaks unless we surrender everything. There is such a relief in giving over the control of our lives into His hands. You and I aren't suited for being in control. God, on the other hand, is perfectly suited for it. We cause ourselves needless turmoil when we get the two roles confused.

Give yourself and everything associated with your life to the One who loves you and knows what is best for you. You are only a steward of all that you have—your resources, your time, your health, your abilities—all of it has been entrusted to you by your Father to manage. Claim no ownership over anything but surrender everything to Him.

Having disavowed ownership of anything in life and acknowledging that everything is His, you will find yourself experiencing freedom from the need to control. You will act responsibly but leave the results to God. You will live each day wisely and productively because the outcome of everything you do will ultimately be His responsibility.

Whatever your age is, be mindful of the fact that your days are numbered. As you submit yourself to Him and realize that life is about experiencing and expressing *agape*, about yielding control of everything to Him and simply living in and from Love, you will gain the wisdom that only comes from Him. And you will make every day count to the fullest.

54

Norman Rockwell Expectations in a Homer Simpson World

There is a river whose streams make glad the city of God,
The holy dwelling places of the Most High.

—Psalm 46:4

I love the paintings of Norman Rockwell. He was known for his illustrations of everyday life during my boyhood and before. When I look at his paintings, they always bring a smile to my heart, if not to my face. There is a pure, innocent simplicity about his work that resonates with memories of days gone by, when life seemed stable and predictable and warm fuzzies abounded in the heart of our nation.

Times, though, have changed. Rockwell died in 1978. Sadly, it seems that for the most part he took the days he portrayed with him. Now we live in a Homer Simpson world. The "aahs" of society seem to have been filled with a constant barrage of "dohs!"

Boys like the Beav and Wally from the old TV program *Leave It to Beaver* respected their parents, girls, their teachers, their neighbors, and even God. Today Bart Simpson has disdain for his dad, Homer, is cleverer than his teachers, dismisses girls, mocks his neighbors, and thinks God is a joke.

I know I must be getting old because I sometimes find myself longing for the good old days and wondering how on earth we've gotten so far off track. The fact is, though, it is what it is, and we might as well learn to deal with it.

Times change. It's that simple. We can fight it or even deny it, but the world we live in isn't a stable place. Thank God, there is a corresponding truth that will sustain us. It's this: Times change, the world changes, but our God never changes.

The Lord is continuously reminding me that I still need to learn more completely who is in control and who isn't. He is and I'm not. What a hard lesson that is to learn! I know it, but I find myself still needing to *know* it. Are you like that?

The bottom line is that we cause ourselves needless stress and grief when we bring our Norman Rockwell expectations into the Homer Simpson world of our daily circumstances. No matter how much we want it to be, life is not a neatly wrapped package with the perfect bow on top. It's messy. It's scary at times. It's unpredictable. And that goes against the grain of our natural desire to be in control of our world.

What's the answer? It is to give up control. To admit we're not in charge and never will be. To know, as counterintuitive as it is, that grace shows up and shows off best in Bart Simpson's hometown of Springfield, not the Beaver's hometown of Mayfield.

It's not an easy pill to swallow, but it's the pill that will lead to spiritual rest and emotional stability. The truth is, I saw the world of Norman Rockwell through a child's eyes. It never was as idyllic as he portrayed. Homer Simpson has always lurked in the shadows. This world is a rollercoaster ride, at least from the human perspective. However, there is a God who loves us passionately and has everything under control.

The psalmist looked beyond the struggles of the ancient world and saw "the city of God." It is to that city that you belong. The apostle Paul wrote, "Our citizenship is in heaven, from which also we eagerly wait for a Savior, the Lord Jesus Christ" (Philippians 3:20).

Grace will empower you to see beyond the disappointments and disillusionments of this world and cause you to see the divine reality that frames everything here. Seeing God in your day-to-day routine will inspire and invigorate you. So yield your expectations to the divine decrees of the One who loves you and gave Himself for you.

55

The Truth Sets You Free

You will know the truth, and the truth will make you free.

—John 8:32

As you seek to grow in your own spiritual development, don't fall for the mistake of thinking that understanding biblical principles or facts is enough to cause you to experience authentic growth. The suggestion that "the truth will make you free" is one whose fallacy can be seen from several vantage points. First and foremost, the problem with the statement is what it leaves out. To suggest that the truth will set you free is only a partial quote from Jesus. What He actually said, in its totality, is "You will know the truth, and the truth will make you free."

Truth alone has no ability to bring about any change in a person's life. The Pharisees proved that. Although they knew the Scriptures as well as anybody in their day, their knowledge of scriptural content did nothing for them. To them, study was an end unto itself. In other words, they studied the Scriptures to know the Scriptures. As strange as it may seem, that is a terrible reason to study the Bible. In fact, it can make a modern-day Pharisee out of you!

We don't study the Bible to learn its contents. We study the Bible to know its Author. It is only as the Scripture leads us into an experiential knowledge of our God that it has fulfilled its purpose in our lives. Remember that Jesus told the Pharisees about the Scriptures, "It is these that testify about Me" (John 5:39). If you've found something other than Jesus Christ through Bible study, you've missed the point. The focal point of the Bible is Jesus Christ Himself! He isn't just "truth" but is "the Truth" that sets us free.

The modern church world has taken the idea that the truth will set us free and has mistakenly come to believe that learning the propositional truths of Scripture will change us. Because of that belief, they've turned the Bible into a handbook of religious guidelines. If you were to ask them if the Bible is simply a book of guidelines for life, most would say no. But watch the way the application of Scripture to people's lives is made in sermons and Bible studies, and you'll come to a different conclusion about what they really believe.

In such sermons and studies there is often much application about what we are to do now but that mentions nothing about knowing our Savior more intimately. Some may call this sort of teaching "practical," but I think a better term for it could be "Christianity Lite" because its emphasis is so heavy on religious performance and so light on Christ Himself.

Many people, unless they are able to find a biblical "principle" of some sort and then show how that principle should guide our actions, think teaching isn't practical. In reality, the demand for "practical teaching" in the church world today masks an underlying urge to *do something* as opposed to *knowing Somebody.*

Now, there's certainly nothing wrong with understanding the practical ways in which Christ wants to express Himself through your daily actions, but here's the problem that often exists: "Biblical principles" are taught in such a way as to suggest that the aim of life is to do right. And nothing could be further from the Truth. Remember, it's about knowing Him. All the "doing" is to flow from that. When we reverse the two, we end up with nothing more than dead religious works, regardless of how admirable they may look to everybody else.

You have not been called to live by biblical truths. You have been called to live by the Truth, who is the Christ who lives inside you. He is your life source, and He wants to animate your daily actions. Your life isn't to be driven by religious determination springing from information you might have learned.

I shudder when I share a message from the Bible that focuses on Jesus Christ and somebody tells me they wished the message had been more "practical." Where did we ever get the idea that telling people what to do is a better way to teach the Bible than showing them who their God is and who they are in Him? Jesus came to reveal the Father to us, not to tell us how to live.

Don't make the mistake of thinking that if you build your lifestyle around biblical principles then you'll experience the life God intends. That's not the way of grace. There are a multitude of religious programs designed to teach you the content of the Bible. We are largely a generation who think that the better we learn the Bible, the better life will be. At the novice end of the spectrum, "Christian education" has become a matter of memorizing Scripture. At the advanced end it's parsing Greek verbs. But if that's the only thing that happens, the result is a person who has some degree of Bible education but still hasn't been set free to really live.

Studying the Bible is not enough. Engage with the Spirit of Christ through the Scripture to find real freedom. Facts only enlighten you. Knowing the Truth will emancipate you!

56

Wounded Soldiers

*If anyone is caught in any trespass, you who are spiritual,
restore such a one in a spirit of gentleness; each one
looking to yourself, so that you too will not be tempted.*

—GALATIANS 6:1

In the midst of armed conflict in Iraq, a young American soldier made a foolish mistake that almost ended his life. It was a mistake that should never have happened. He should have known better. He had been taught the rules of engagement for battle. In basic training, his instructors had drilled him again and again on how to handle such circumstances as those he faced in Iraq. He had even memorized the proper protocol from his manual and could recite it without so much as a slight hesitation.

In the heat of battle, all of his training had seemed to go out the window. In a moment of carelessness, he acted the wrong way and was injured—seriously.

"You're going home, son," he was told by his superior in the field hospital. "Your service to your country is appreciated. You risked your life here today and have paid a price. On behalf of your president and a proud country, thank you."

When the young man returned to his small hometown, a celebration awaited him. The people were proud that their own boy had fought on the front line. At church on the Sunday after his return home, he received special recognition in a service where the congregation honored him. He was called a hero, a brave soldier, and a true patriot. A local reporter was there and wrote an article that appeared in the paper the following day: "Young Hero Honored," the headline read.

That's how they all saw him. Nobody disputed it.

There was another young man from that same congregation. He had become a Christian there after years of addiction to alcohol and drugs. The transformation was amazing. The church nurtured him, loved him. It was in that church that he began to sense an inward stirring to go to seminary and prepare for lifelong service as a pastor.

During the years he was in seminary, his church supported him financially and with their encouragement. They knew that he was being taught how to live the life of a pastor. He was learning how to offer spiritual guidance to others. They couldn't have been more proud.

Then one day, a leader in the church received a telephone call from him. The news that followed was devastating. The young man began to pour out his story…of how he had been having marital problems. He told about how his grades had been slipping. He had been working a full 40 hours a week at night while attending school full-time.

And somehow in the midst of it all, he had allowed himself to slip back into old drinking patterns. Nobody had known about his relapse until a few nights before, when he was stopped by the police and arrested for drunk driving. An article on page 2 in the local newspaper the next day read, "Local Seminarian Arrested."

Within 24 hours, he was expelled from the seminary. Devastated, he explained his decision to move back home with his family. "We will be moving in with my wife's parents for a few weeks while we find a place to live," he said. "I'll plan to see you at church on Sunday." When the church leader hung up the phone, he was stunned.

How do you imagine the events of the following weeks unfolding in this young man's home church? How do you think he would be received when he came back to the church that week? What words would your church use to describe this young seminarian? Would it be the same words they would use to describe the soldier?

Consider these similarities between them: 1) Both the soldier and the seminarian had been trained for handling front line battle situations. 2) They were both fighting for a noble cause. 3) They both knew how they should respond in circumstances where they were at risk. 4) They both failed because they didn't practice what they had been taught. 5) They both came back home to their church.

Would you receive them back home in the same way? What would you say to the soldier? To the seminarian? Do you believe that to call the young man who failed to live up to his training as a soldier a "hero" is inappropriate? Wouldn't this be likely to cause other soldiers to conclude that it really doesn't matter whether they live up to their training and position as soldiers? Would it encourage carelessness among the ranks? Would it give them a "license" to be poor soldiers?

There are many who have been on the front lines of spiritual service who have been wounded—and of those, many have been injured because of their own foolishness. How are we to handle those who have deliberately made wrong choices?

The Bible offers a few examples. How did the father of the prodigal receive his son who had intentionally chosen the far country? How did Jesus respond to the woman caught in the very act of adultery?

How do you handle those who have made wrong choices?

Are we to be "soft on sin"? Of course not. But we are to be soft on *people*. Those who have been wounded don't need our scorn. They need our sympathy. Defeated soldiers have rehearsed their failure in their own minds a thousand times. They haven't "gotten away with" anything. Sin still brings its own punishment. They don't need that from us. What they do need is love, not lectures. They need acceptance, not accusations.

Pray and ask the Lord to bring to mind a soldier of Jesus Christ you know who has been wounded in battle. Then pray for that person. Maybe it would be good to call them or visit them and let them know you love them. Remember, the only way a soldier ever gets hurt in combat is if he was actually in the battle. Those who never go to the front lines won't suffer combat injuries. Only those who face the enemy up close and personal run that risk.

Some may come home bloody and broken. But remember—they were in the fight. How they are received at home may set the course for the rest of their lives. Reach out today to someone and be among the minority— those who show love and prove they actually care. That's what grace does.

57

Monkey Gods

Of His fullness we have all received, and grace upon grace.

—John 1:16

When Melanie and I were in India, the same taxi driver drove us around town for several days. He was a nice young man who willingly answered any question we had about Indian culture. Over a period of a few days, I really came to like him.

It was on a Saturday that we were in his taxi going from Kota to the city of Agra, where we were going to see the Taj Mahal. As lunchtime drew near, I asked him if he knew a good place along our route where we could stop to eat. He did, and it wasn't long until we pulled up in front of the restaurant.

Since I'd known him for a few days and liked him, I invited him to come in and let me buy lunch for him. "No, thank you," he replied. "Are you sure?" I asked. "I really would like to buy your lunch today." "I appreciate it," he said, "but I'm fasting today."

We went in and ate without him, and when we returned to the car, I asked him about his fast. I learned that he was fasting to the monkey god Hanuman. Monkeys are greatly revered in India. You see them everywhere. They are given free rein of the place and come and go anywhere as they please.

He explained a little of the history of Hanuman to me and then I said to him, "You know I like you, don't you?" "Yes," he said. "You are a nice man." "Then may I ask you a question and know that you'll understand I mean no offense by it?" I asked. "Of course," he answered. So I looked him straight in the eyes and asked, "When you're fasting and praying—now, be honest with me—do you ever think to yourself, *I'm praying to a monkey!*"

He smiled and said, "I understand why you would ask that question, but you see, our culture is different from yours. We are taught how to live out our religion from the time we are small children. We are taught not to question it, but to just do it. So I don't think about it. I just do what I've been taught to do."

As the week progressed, I did talk to him about Jesus Christ and he listened very politely. Like many in India, he was respectful enough of me that if I'd had a carving of Jesus he would have been willing to put it up on his altar at home and pray to Jesus right along with all the other gods he offered prayers to. Of course, you know that shows he didn't understand the gospel.

As time has passed, I've come to recognize that the young man's attitude exists even in the Christian church. There are things many of us were taught as we grew up that are simply wrong. Many people who sit in church every week have horribly faulty ideas about who God is, about who they are, and about what He expects from them.

They go through the motions of their religious rituals in an effort to please a God who already is pleased with them because they are in His Beloved Son, in whom He is well pleased. But they think that if they don't do the right things, He will curse them, and if they do the right things, He will bless them. They think they are rotten people who need God's help to improve themselves and they are constantly trying to do just that. They believe that God has high demands on them concerning what they do, what they say, and even what they think. They believe that bad things happen when they fall short in those areas.

The truth of the gospel of grace is that God loves you. He accepts you just like you are. That doesn't mean that He won't change your attitudes and actions over time, but that's His job, not yours. Your responsibility is to yield yourself to Him in faith that He will transform you by His grace, in His time and in His way.

It's true that contemporary Christians aren't praying to a monkey god, but many are stubbornly holding on to old beliefs just because it's what they have always believed. It would never occur to them to question those beliefs.

The fact of the matter is, if you are going to grow and go on in your grace walk, there will be things at times you must reconsider—things you must subject to the Scripture as if you were learning them for the first time. To walk in freedom, there are things you may need to reject, to put out of your belief system and your actions.

Have you changed spiritually in the past years? Months? Weeks? Remember that growing things always change. Don't allow old viewpoints to become an issue of idolatry in your life. Submit yourself, your views, and your actions to the Holy Spirit and ask Him to show you the truth. Be willing to think about what you believe and do, and be willing to ask yourself why in light of God's Word. That's how you'll grow and how you'll experience your freedom in Christ. Dead religious tradition becomes stagnant, but in the fullness of His life you can experience grace upon grace.

58

The Danger of Drifting

*We must pay much closer attention to what we
have heard, so that we do not drift away from it.*

—Hebrews 2:1

One of the things I learned when I was taking sailing classes was to determine my course using a protractor and a chart. When sailing, it's important to realize that if you plan to go a long way, you'd better be sure you aren't off course a few degrees when you begin. If you are, you're going to end up in big trouble later.

Being a few degrees off course in the beginning doesn't look too serious, but the longer you sail, the further you move away from your intended destination. Imagine an angle that keeps getting wider and wider as it moves away from its originating point and you'll understand the importance of not missing your bearing by a few degrees when sailing.

The same is true in your grace walk. When your eyes were opened to the gospel and you began to follow Christ, that wasn't the finish line, but was the starting point of your journey.

Paul begins all his epistles with the word *grace* because that is where we have to start if we want to end up where our hearts long to be and at the destination our Father has determined for us. If you start your faith journey at the point of grace and move forward charting your course by grace, you will move further and further into the waters of abundant living. Paul typically also ended his epistles with the word *grace*. The grace of God is to be our starting point and our final destination. In between, it is to be grace all the way.

If, however, you start from a place of grace but begin to drift toward legalism, you will most certainly end up in a place of frustration and defeat in your life. Many Christians have started well but have drifted away from a grace walk and have found themselves in the troubled waters of legalism.

I actually got lost at sea once because I got off course. We were in the British Virgin Islands, and my plan was to go from one side of the island of Virgin Gorda around the northern tip and arrive at beautiful Cane Garden Bay on the other side. It didn't work out that way. A storm came in between our boat and land. For hours and hours we saw no land at all. When I finally spotted land again, I couldn't figure out where I was because I had completely lost my bearings. Eventually I made contact with a cruise ship, whose captain sent the Coast Guard to rescue us.

Once I saw land again, though, a strange thing happened to my perception. I would study the chart and compare it to the land on the horizon, and I'd become convinced I had the correct bearings again. I would see the markings for an outcropping of rocks or a sheer cliff on the chart and would then look toward the land—and I would find a feature that looked to me exactly like what I was seeing on the chart. The problem was, I wasn't really seeing what the chart showed. I was deceiving myself into thinking I was because it made me feel better to believe that I wasn't really off course. Sometimes when we drift away we tend to misjudge where we actually are. We may tell ourselves we aren't that far off course and it's not that serious. We may even convince ourselves we aren't off course at all, and what we're experiencing is simply a part of the journey. In time, however, we will come to discover that our wandering off course can bring devastating consequences if we don't correct it. Sometimes we may even need others to help us rediscover our original course.

I started well, but I drifted off course. The same thing has happened to many who follow Jesus. A man at a conference where I had just spoken said to me, "I didn't have to be taught grace when I first trusted Christ. That's how I naturally lived. I had to be taught legalism. Then the things

I had done in the beginning because I wanted to became things I should do, and that's when it all unraveled."

He's right. It made me think of Paul's words to the Galatians: "You started out well. Who has hindered you?" Staying on course with grace must be intentional, because the current of dead religion always pushes against grace.

A life in grace is one where we are carried along by the wind (the Spirit) and navigate our way through the water (the Word). We must set the sails of our life in such a way that the Spirit carries us along the course He has set for us as we experience the Living Word, Jesus Christ Himself. If we become distracted from Him by the undertow of religious demands, our journey can be unfulfilling at best and disastrous at worst.

Set your course in life today by the love and grace of God. Pay close attention to what you have heard and know to be true about your journey of grace. Be careful not to drift away from Him into a religious lifestyle that will lead you in a wrong direction. If you see that you've gotten off course, make the necessary tack to get back on course again. If you need help, don't be too proud to ask others…you may be in a situation where failing to do so could lead to shipwreck.

59

A Subtle Form of Idolatry

*"Not by might nor by power, but by My
Spirit," says the LORD of hosts.*

—ZECHARIAH 4:6

It happens every year during Easter Week in the Philippines, especially in the Pampanga Province. Some there relive the story of the passion of Christ in an attempt to feel closer to God. On Good Friday, they march down the street scourging their own backs with instruments that cut their flesh. Over a dozen people are actually hung on crosses, some with rope and others actually nailed.

They aren't left there to die but are taken down after a time. Most participants attest to a feeling of having been forgiven and made clean by the rituals. They readily affirm that their goal was to be involved in atonement for their sins. Ironically, they don't understand that when any person believes that he has a part in obtaining forgiveness from God for his sins, he has committed a form of idolatry.

Idolatry takes place when people revere anything above or even equally to God. If we believe that our own works have any part in obtaining the forgiveness that has actually been given to us as a result of what Jesus and He alone has done, we exalt our own work to the status of God. Forgiveness is through Christ and Christ alone. When we add anything to it, we have diluted and thus destroyed the essence of the good news of grace.

The fanatic religious idolatry of self-flagellation or self-imposed crucifixion is probably obvious to you, but there is a way that many believers have unknowingly fallen into a kind of idolatry that can fit in that same category. It is commonly called "rededicating myself to Christ."

That term is normally associated with asking God to forgive us of the things we've done wrong and promising, with His help, to do better. The rededication may involve a promise to read the Bible more consistently, pray more earnestly, witness more boldly, give more generously, avoid sin more passionately, or some other action that is probably dictated by the church culture that shaped our thinking.

The whole concept is that we try harder to do better in an attempt to become a better person. It is a religious mixture of self-help combined with prayers for a divine boost to enable us to follow through. On the surface it may look commendable, but in reality it is exactly opposite from what the Bible teaches us to do.

The reality is that Jesus has never once called on us to rededicate ourselves. Instead He says that we should renounce our self-effort to do better and simply follow (live out of our union) Him. Jesus said in Matthew 16:24, "If anyone wishes to come after Me, he must deny himself, and take up his cross and follow Me."

Note that He said to "deny" yourself, not "dedicate" yourself. Rededication generally focuses on bringing our behavior up to par. Consequently, the focus of our lives becomes ourselves and how we behave. This sort of idolatry exalts our own efforts to live a holy lifestyle above the God who dwells in us. It takes our focus off the only One who can consistently live a lifestyle that honors our Father, and it puts the spotlight on us and what we can do to improve.

Embrace this practice and it will cause you to constantly stare at yourself to see how well you're doing. It will cause you to invest all your attention and energy in improving your actions. As horrifying as the thought may be to you, it will eventually cause you to love yourself more than Christ—the evidence will be the enormous attention and energy you will end up spending on yourself and what you are doing or not doing. Live in the subtle trap of idolatrous rededication and eventually *you* will come first, not Christ. You'll spend your time either feeling self-condemnation for not doing better or religious pride because of how well you think you're doing.

Whatever we put before God is an idol. That includes our own attempt to do better, thinking it will make us be better. If you make your own demand for better religious behavior the priority of your life, that is a not-so-subtle form of idolatry. It forces Christ into the background and puts your own behavior front and center.

Your grace walk isn't about you and how well you behave. It's about having an intimate love relationship with God through Christ. Where is your focus? Is it on you? On what you're doing or not doing? Or are your attention and devotion squarely focused on Jesus Christ?

There is a real need for repentance in the modern church. The biblical meaning of repentance is to change our minds. We need to change our minds when it comes to this idolatrous practice of rededicating ourselves to live for God. Genuine repentance recognizes the need to turn away from ourselves and our never-ending, never-satisfied demand for perfect behavior. It is the need for a turning to Jesus Christ. He will become the catalyst and foundation upon which improvement in our behavior will come.

We must stop worshipping the false god of our own behavioral expectations. Stop worshipping our self-efforts to improve. We must stop permitting our walk with Christ to be about *my* efforts, *my* sins, *my* good works, *my* promises to do better. It's not about me, me, me. Christianity is all Him, Him, Him!

May God grant the gift of repentance to His church so that we will quit worshipping ourselves at the Temple of Rededication. May we turn to Him and acknowledge that we will never be able to live up to our own self-righteous demands, so we are casting ourselves on His grace and love. Then, and only then, will we find that Christ and Christ alone is our Deliverer. He will free us from being held hostage in a prison of perpetual rededication. When we turn away from rededication and turn to Him, we will hear Him lovingly whisper, "I never intended for you to change yourself. I just want you to rest here in My arms. I'll bring about the changes in your life. You just stay here and enjoy Me."

60

The Value of Laughter

The joy of the LORD is your strength.

—NEHEMIAH 8:10

When Nehemiah led the people of Israel to rebuild the wall around Jerusalem, a ceremony was held after the reconstruction was complete. Ezra the priest stood before the people and began to read the Law of God to them. As he read, the people were moved to tears and began to weep as they worshipped God. Nehemiah encouraged them with these words: "Do not be grieved, for the joy of the LORD is your strength" (Nehemiah 8:10).

Finding strength in joy is something that children naturally experience. I remember such a joy I experienced as a young boy. It was a new pair of tennis shoes. Paul Parrot Shoes sold a pair that had the personal guarantee of a talking parrot on the television commercial. Not only would he give you a free plastic egg filled with candy, but this parrot assured young customers that his shoes would "make your feet run faster, as fast as I can fly."

On one occasion when my parents bought me a pair of shoes, I begged for Paul Parrot Shoes. When I got those shoes home, I put them on, laced them up, and went outside to try them out. I timed myself as I ran completely around my house. It was true! I could feel the strength these shoes were giving me. I laughed out loud as I imagined Paul Parrot himself trying to keep up if he were flying beside me. It was my fastest speed ever around my house. I had never actually timed myself before, but it didn't matter. I just knew this was a record.

Do you want to find strength to "run and not grow weary" (Isaiah 40:31 NIV)? Then resolve to laugh and have fun. If anybody has a reason to do so, you do. The party in the kingdom of God is going on right now. Don't be like the older brother in the story of the prodigal son, who stood outside and missed the fun. He was so obsessed with the rules that there was no place in his paradigm for partying.

His father obviously didn't share that somber outlook. When the prodigal son came home, the father insisted that it was *right* to throw a party, given the circumstances. He knew that his returning son would be strengthened and validated as a son through such a celebration. He knew everybody else would see the outrageous, over-the-top kind of love he had for his son. He knew the family and farmhands would all be better off through the party—that they would be strengthened and encouraged. He knew that joy would become their strength.

Come on in to the ongoing gospel party and watch your own strength grow. In the face of life's stressful moments, a good laugh in the Spirit of joy can bring strength that nothing else can. Laugh at life. Laugh with friends. Laugh over your faith. Even laugh at yourself.

Laughing at ourselves is a healthy part of a godly lifestyle because it reminds us that life doesn't have to be taken so seriously. It has the effect of a good dose of medicine. I have often laughed at my own weaknesses— my terrible sense of direction, my pathetic lack of mechanical skills—not to mention many other things I'm not secure enough to tell you right now!

Topping the list of causes to laugh at myself are the foolish things I have mistakenly said. There was the time in church after I had spoken when I wanted everybody to stand to their feet and bow their heads for prayer. That's what I wanted. What I said was, "Will you please stand with your head bowed to your feet?"

Later, some people told me they thought I was beginning some sort of aerobics ministry right there on the spot. We all had a good laugh, especially me.

Learn to laugh at your own idiosyncrasies and mistakes, and you'll discover you can create a joyful atmosphere that's literally refreshing.

What makes you laugh? One medical study done at Stanford

University Medical School reported that the average kindergarten student laughs 300 times a day. Yet adults average just 17 laughs a day. Could this have something to with what Jesus said—that in order to enter the kingdom of God we must become like little children?

Growing in grace will cause you to laugh more. The blessings of God in our lives are enough to make us laugh with joy when we see them. When the nation of Israel was delivered from captivity, the psalmist described their response: "Then our mouth was filled with laughter and our tongue with joyful shouting" (Psalm 126:2).

Have you allowed yourself to become bogged down in adult concerns to the point that you've lost the laughter in your life? Perhaps one of the greatest spiritual benefits you could experience is to learn to laugh again. Don't take life (or yourself) too seriously.

Laughter disarms your critics, boosts your immune system, dissolves stress, anxiety, irritation, anger, grief, and depression. It reduces pain, develops your sense of humor, brings balance to your life, and can even be like a small amount of exercise.

Pray and ask that the gift of laughter will grow in you. Then, when you sense a laugh rising up from within you, don't squelch it. Laugh loud. Laugh long. Laugh hard. Remember, you are never in greater touch with the climate of heaven than when you express joyful laughter.

A Word from the Author

If reading *The Grace Walk Devotional* has encouraged you, I would be happy to hear from you. Our purpose at Grace Walk Ministries is to share the liberating message of what it means to be in Christ and have Him live His life through us each day. We share this message through teaching in local settings, through radio, television, the Internet, books, audio-video resources, and mission outreaches.

At the time of this publication, Grace Walk Ministries has offices in the U.S., Canada, Mexico, Pakistan, Australia, Argentina, and El Salvador. Our leadership team members are all great communicators and are passionate about sharing the message of our God's loving grace. If you would be interested in having any of our team or me speak to your church or group, please feel free to contact us at the address below.

I also invite you to visit our website at www.gracewalk.org, where you can learn more about our mission and how we are carrying it out across the world. On the home page of our website, you can also watch "Sunday Preaching," a Bible teaching I share each week that remains available online throughout that week.

You may contact me as follows:

> Dr. Steve McVey
> Grace Walk Ministries
> PO Box 3669
> Riverview, FL 33568
> Phone: 800-472-2311
> E-mail: info@gracewalk.org
> Web address: www.gracewalk.org

May God continue to bless you in your own grace walk as you come to "know Him and the power of His resurrection and the fellowship of His sufferings" (Philippians 3:10).

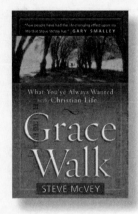

Grace Walk
What You've Always Wanted in the Christian Life

Nothing you have ever done, nothing you could ever do, will match the incomparable joy of letting Jesus live His life through you. It is what makes the fire of passion burn so brightly in new believers. And it is what causes the light of contentment to shine in the eyes of mature believers who are growing in grace.

As you relax in Jesus and delight in His love and friendship, you'll find that He will do more *through you* and *in you* than you could ever do for Him or for yourself. Today is the day to let go of doing and start *being* who you are. Today is the day to start experiencing the grace walk.

The Grace Walk Experience
Enjoying Life the Way God Intends

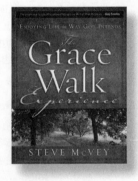

"Make sure you're in the Word." "Have a quiet time every day." "Rededicate yourself." "Make a commitment." "Just stop sinning!" Your frustration may be the catalyst God wants to use—right here, right now—to give you a gloriously new understanding of the Christian walk.

Take a deep breath and relax through eight weekly, interactive studies from Steve McVey that show you...

- why it's all right to give up on yourself and your efforts
- how to leave behind a performance- and fear-based faith
- ways to quit "doing" for God, so He can live through you
- how to view the Bible, salvation, and evangelism from a new perspective
- how to be free to enjoy God and the abundant life He's given you

Superb for small-group discussions, church classes, and individual study.

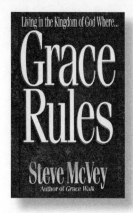

Living in the Kingdom of God Where…
Grace Rules

Are you "living by the rules"…or are you letting God's grace rule you?

There's a big difference. If you're living *for* God—living by the rules—you'll always be exhausted. You'll feel as if you're not doing enough for Him…and that if you don't "measure up," He'll be displeased with you.

But God never meant for you to live the Christian life that way! His love for you isn't based on how you perform for Him. He sent Christ to set you free from rules. He didn't call you to serve Him in your own feeble power…but to let *His* limitless power flow through you!

What's more, this power is available to you right now. God has provided everything you need for a truly meaningful, joy-filled life here on earth…all because of His marvelous grace. Find out how to rest in that grace and let Him live through you in *Grace Rules*.

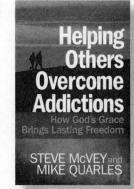

Helping Others Overcome Addictions
How God's Grace Brings Lasting Freedom
Steve McVey and Mike Quarles

Immerse yourself in the basic, addiction-breaking truths of God's Word! If you want to effectively help someone, or if you yourself are struggling, the authors show you how freedom from addiction is found only when people

- fully believe what God says about who they are
- move beyond the 12-Step concept of inescapable "addict identity"
- stop harboring unforgiveness, understand what it means to be radically right with God, and dwell in who they are in Christ

In this book you'll see that freedom from addiction is found not in a program, but in a Person—Jesus, God's Son, the One who can truly set people free. *Includes helpful material on codependency, as well as advice for setting up recovery/ support groups for those gaining freedom from addictive behavior.*